People Express

Philip Whiteley

- Fast track route to fail-safe strategies for managing people

- Covers all the key aspects of people management, particularly the rapid changes of recent years as skill requirements have grown and the concept of intellectual capital has taken hold

- Examples and lessons from some of the world's most successful people businesses, including IBM Europe, Southwest Airlines and Parker Hannifin, and ideas from the smartest thinkers, including Jeffrey Pfeffer, Mark Huselid, David Ulrich and Leif Edvinsson

- Includes a glossary of key concepts and a comprehensive resources guide

PEOPLE 09.01

>> EXPRESS EXEC. COM <<

essential management thinking at your fingertips

First published 2002 by
Capstone Publishing (a Wiley company)
8 Newtec Place
Magdalen Road
Oxford OX4 1RE
United Kingdom
http://www.capstoneideas.com

CIP catalogue records for this book are available from the British Library and the US Library of Congress

ISBN 1-84112-211-4

This book is printed on acid-free paper

Substantial discounts on bulk quantities of Capstone books are available to corporations, professional associations and other organizations. Please contact Capstone for more details on +44 (0)1865 798 623 or (fax) +44 (0)1865 240 941 or (e-mail) info@wiley-capstone.co.uk

Contents

Introduction to ExpressExec

ExpressExec is 3 million words of the latest management thinking compiled into 10 modules. Each module contains 10 individual titles forming a comprehensive resource of current business practice written by leading practitioners in their field. From brand management to balanced scorecard, ExpressExec enables you to grasp the key concepts behind each subject and implement the theory immediately. Each of the 100 titles is available in print and electronic formats.

Through the ExpressExec.com Website you will discover that you can access the complete resource in a number of ways:

» printed books or e-books;
» e-content – PDF or XML (for licensed syndication) adding value to an intranet or Internet site;
» a corporate e-learning/knowledge management solution providing a cost-effective platform for developing skills and sharing knowledge within an organization;
» bespoke delivery – tailored solutions to solve your need.

Why not visit www.expressexec.com and register for free key management briefings, a monthly newsletter and interactive skills checklists. Share your ideas about ExpressExec and your thoughts about business today.

Please contact elound@wiley-capstone.co.uk for more information.

Introduction to People Express

» Research indicates that people matters are of integral importance to business decision-making, not a separate welfare matter.
» There is the birth of a new strand of management thinking in the USA, viewing the organization as human and organic, not mechanical; this book charts the rise of such thinking alongside similar models from Germany, Sweden, and Japan.

Recent years have seen increasing debates over the future of management. The political triumphs of capitalism, and the dominance of the Anglo-Saxon model within capitalism, have seen the concept of enriching shareholders as a dominant driving force.

The backlash against this view is seen not only in the protestors at G-8 summit meetings and other similar gatherings, but also in the campaigns of trade unions and many politicians who argue for a "stakeholder" approach where profitability is just one objective, alongside care for the environment, customers, and employees.

Research shows that organizations that treat all their stakeholders well, including their employees, also return more to shareholders (see Chapter 6 and Chapter 9, "Links with business performance"). This places the management of the people that comprise an organization at the heart of decision-making, regardless of one's preferred model, especially as skill requirements increase in the knowledge economy. In business, people count, and those who have neglected this have struggled, as hasty mergers or excessive downsizing or poor health and safety records have ruined reputations, demoralized workforces, and weakened an organization's effectiveness. At the same time, the new accounting discipline of intellectual capital has emerged in the past ten years to try to give managers some means of gauging the asset represented in the know-how and ability of their people.

It is a fairly simple observation to note that organizations comprise people, but some management theories have categorized people issues, normally called human resources management or HRM, in a separate bundle, and described the constituent parts of the organization as "units," made up of "headcount," to be moved about, merged or de-merged at will.

An increasing strand of thinking challenges this: it argues that the organization is organic, not mechanical; that people are unpredictable, not blindly obedient; that engagement and commitment are fundamental, not an added ingredient. It follows from this that all management is a form of people management, and that the different aspects of the discipline explored in the *People Express* series are of fundamental concern to the functioning and well-being of the organization. The recent history of HRM principally concerns the rise of such thinking. This book explores this, alongside other models developed – particularly those in Germany, Sweden, and Japan – and analyzes their strengths and weaknesses, and relevance for contemporary organizations.

The specialist areas focused on in the other nine books in this series are:

» Global Human Resources;
» Online People Strategies;
» Recruitment and Retention;
» Teamworking;
» Managing Diversity;
» Motivation;
» Managing the Flexible Workforce;
» Performance and Reward Management; and
» Training and Development.

This work looks at the changing status and influence of such matters in the wider scheme of business management.

People Express: What is People Management?

» People management falls into an uneasy category within management: on the one hand it is seen as a specialism in its own right but,
on the other hand, some aspects are common to all managers, as all
have people reporting to them.
» Personnel, or human resources, did not fit neatly into the departments
of the conventional twentieth-century corporation.
» Good management of people is not the same as having a strong
personnel department.
» The growth of teamworking, alliances and more porous organizational structures, together with the rise of intangible assets, offer
opportunities for people management to become more central.

"The day we screw up the people thing, the company is over."
Jack Welch, chairman and CEO, General Electric

People management may equally be termed personnel, human resources or human relations. The very existence of a list of terms, and uncertainty over which to use, is symptomatic of an uneasy relationship between this discipline and general management.

Compared with marketing, branding or financial control, there is no universal term and there has been some debate over whether it could be said to constitute a distinct strand of management with a discrete body of knowledge. More professional management qualifications and associations in human resources management have been established recently in personnel management than in accountancy-related or engineering professions. Yet the lack of a deeply rooted professional identity to the task of managing people is, paradoxically, a symptom of its importance. Managing people is something that every manager does, so it cannot be regarded simply as a specialism.

The strands within people management, as represented in the *People Express* series are: recruitment and retention; teamworking; managing diversity; motivation; flexible working; performance and reward management; and training and development. To reflect globalization and the rise of the Internet, we also include the categories of global human resources and online people strategies. All managers will have a say in recruiting their team members – sometimes an exclusive say. All will care about the teamwork, motivation, and pay of people who are their closest colleagues and who are responsible for executing the manager's aims. The more enlightened ones may also care about diversity and learning opportunities.

There is also an increasing amount of research indicating that it is the motivation, skills, and teamwork of a company's staff that make the decisive difference in the success of the organization (see Chapter 9, "Links with business performance" and *Motivation Express*).

Given this intrinsic link between human resources management and the rest of the business, personnel management has not fitted easily into the rigid departments that have characterized most organizations in the past 100 years. To fit this structure, a personnel or human resources department has had to sit in the background, busying itself with the minutiae of employment contracts, payroll, recruitment forms, and the grievance and disciplinary procedures. When it has ventured out and proposed a learning or appraisal scheme, which it says line managers ought to carry out, the busy line managers may not have fully understood the rationale; in turn, the personnel managers have not fully understood the jobs people are doing, the process has failed to add much value to the business, and the department has, understandably, returned to its administrative tasks. In such organizations the success or otherwise of people management rests largely upon the aptitude and skills for such a task that the individual line managers have. The most effective support the company can offer is in training the managers in these tasks.

There is an increasing awareness that HR departments that try to break out of this cycle must understand and learn the business first. If not, they will be foisting solutions that may bear little relation to people's real needs. There is now a wide array – arguably too wide – of personnel-related "solutions," from personality tests through competency frameworks to 360-degree appraisals, which consultancies and some HR departments are all too willing to encourage line managers to implement. Some thinkers argue that this "addiction to tools" creates a vicious circle for HR managers: the less time they spend understanding the business and imposing such tools, the more respect they will lose from line managers, and the more they will have to seek ever increasingly intricate HR tools.

Good management of people is therefore not the same thing as having a strong personnel department. Some companies, such as easyJet in the UK, have recorded impressive growth employing well-motivated staff without a human resources manager – at least in the formative years. Leadership is increasingly seen as playing a key part. Like Virgin, Hewlett Packard and Southwest Airlines, easyJet has a charismatic founder whom the staff respect. A survey by the Hay Group in 2001 found that successful entrepreneurs are people of high integrity who believe in treating staff well.

Senior managers can also change their approaches to personnel with the business cycle. Many regard human resources initiatives as a "good thing to do," but often only when business is good, and sometimes without understanding the dynamics involved. They will still seek to reduce headcount whenever cost savings need to be found, at which point personnel managers are the unwilling executioners, calling in staff to hand them their redundancy notices.

THE SEPARATE DEPARTMENT'S DAYS ARE NUMBERED

Personnel management cannot continue in a separate silo, however. Technology is taking the administrative role away from the personnel department. Intranets can handle most routine bureaucracy concerned with keeping employees' records up to date – the staff can even enter in many of the details themselves. Recruitment and much training, particularly training that is rich in facts and data, can be carried out online (see Chapter 4). Led by BP-Amoco, corporations have begun outsourcing such administration on a massive scale. Personnel managers either have a future as business people helping teams manage people and get the best out of them; or they run an outsourced administrative function; or they do not have a future.

Some thinkers have gone so far as to say that the large corporation, with its massive, specialist departments, was a twentieth-century phenomenon. If this is exaggerated, it is nonetheless certain that cross-disciplinary teamworking within organizations, strategic alliances between them, and outsourcing will continue apace, together with the rise of skilled professionals who operate as independent businesses bringing with them their social networks.

The rise of knowledge management and intellectual capital also pushes the matter of people management up the agenda for executives. Some commentators dismiss these approaches as fads, or as perhaps only relevant for high-tech companies with highly skilled individuals and knowledge that can be quantified. Such an easy dismissal misses a wider point, however. At some point in the early 1990s the proportion of a company's market value taken up by intangible assets overtook that accounted for by fixed assets.[1] This is a profound change, the effects of which are only just beginning to be reflected in managerial emphasis. Put simply, the annual accounts of a modern company only record between 1 percent and 25 percent of assets; the rest is intangible. Attempts have been made to codify intangibles into such categories as ways of working, processes or the brand, but at root they reflect the collective skills and talents of the organization's people.

One implication is that calculations on cost savings from redundancy programs are increasingly inaccurate if companies do not bother to gauge the value of the skills they are losing, which they may not be able to attract once business picks up. Even without such measurements, a few companies have sought to hold on to their staff during a downturn, even if there is little work for them to do.

Intellectual capital has moved out of the laboratory. Around 200 companies now use a calibration of their intellectual capital under the model devised by Leif Edvinsson (an explanation can be read at www.intellectualcapital.se and this is discussed further in the section on "Intellectual capital," Chapter 6; see also the case study of Skandia, Chapter 7).

The development throws up new challenges, and arguably a new profession. Is someone who measures a company's intellectual capital an accountant, a human resources professional, a statistician, or a combination of all three?

Another new term that has entered managerial lexicon in the past decade is "learning organization." As with intellectual capital, it runs the risk of being interpreted in a superficial way but possesses an underlying logic. Organizational requirements change continually as markets and technology change, and people are required to adapt. Unskilled jobs are continually replaced by skilled jobs, and professional bodies encourage their members to engage in continuous professional development, rather than regarding their qualifications as being the summit of their learning career.

These developments in business priorities and organization, together with the research evidence mentioned above, offer tremendous opportunities for people management – or whatever it will be called – to come of age.

KEY LEARNING POINTS

» There is uncertainty over the correct term for people management, and whether it comprises a discrete body of knowledge.
» Some degree of management of people is universal to all managers.

» Personnel management has not fitted easily into conventional departmental structures, and has not always been perceived to add value, despite its potential.

» Approaches need to be rooted in the business, not comprising human resources "tools" bought off the shelf.

» New technology is freeing administrative human resources managers and the concept of intellectual capital is gaining ground. These developments make people management more strategic.

NOTE

1 Ernst & Young (1997), *Measures that Matter*. Ernst & Young.

The Evolution of People Management

» Modern history of people management begins with the philan-
  thropy of the nineteenth century, which became the welfare-based
  personnel department of the twentieth century. Mary Parker Follett
  was an early prophet of partnership.
» By the mid twentieth century, scientific management holds sway;
  sees people as cost; personnel department is separate from general
  management and largely consumed with administration. Employees
  seek protection through law and trade unions, not through their
  employers.
» Japanese manufacturers adopt different approach, with practice of
  senior managers having experience in personnel. Germany also
  developed a distinctive post-war history with works councils taking
  over part of personnel function.
» Introduction of human resources in 1980s at first reinforces scientific
  management, but the 1990s see moves towards strategic role.

"Drive out fear so that everyone may work effectively for the company because they want it to succeed."

W. Edwards Deming

Management of people is as old as work itself. While most forms of the profession apply only to modern organizations, a key part – training – can be assumed to go back to earliest societies. The start of its modern history can be traced to the medieval guilds, which established the apprenticeship system where young recruits were bound to masters as they learned their craft. Indeed, the spread of industrialization appeared to be regressive for training as a profession, as many new jobs were considerably less skilled than those that they replaced. Skilled operatives in northern England in the early nineteenth century, known as Luddites, risked the death penalty to protest against the new machines that took away their jobs and their crafts. Activity was particularly centered on the weaving trades.[1]

In the nineteenth century, the early years of industrialization, employee welfare and development was primarily the concern of the factory proprietor, although minimal statutory protection outlawing slavery and child labor was introduced. Some benevolent proprietors, such as Titus Salt and Robert Owen in the UK, created their own "model" villages for staff, featuring better wages and housing, which have been the subject of extensive study. This age also saw the rise of socialism and trade unions, which increasingly sought radical alternatives to profit-making enterprises either peacefully, in the cooperative movement, or violently, through revolution. As such, there was a divorce between working-class movements, and efforts to improve motivation and welfare within capitalist organizations.

This split became entrenched when, in the 1890s, small, medium, and large-scale organizations began applying Frederick Taylor's theory of "scientific management," which viewed employees as primarily a means to a profitable end, to be motivated only by pay or the fear of discipline. After four years as chief engineer at the Midvale steelworks in Philadelphia, during which time he introduced time-and-motion study to the workplace, Taylor became an independent consultant in 1893 and published *The Principles of Scientific Management* in 1911.

Voices dissenting from this confrontational, highly politicized situation were rare. However, one that stood out in the early part of the twentieth century was that of the prophetic Mary Parker Follett. In the current context of the deliberate breaking-down of departmental silos by modern organizations and the fostering of interdisciplinary teamwork, it is timely to record her observations:

> "I think we should un-departmentalize our thinking in regard to every problem that comes to us. I do not think that we have psychological and ethical and economic problems. We have human problems, with psychological, ethical and economical aspects."[2]

Although Parker Follett was a well-regarded public speaker and prolific author, it is probably fair to say that her ideas were not widely embraced by managers. If they had, the industrial and political history of the twentieth century would have been very different. She preached partnership at a time when managers treated trade unions as havens for Communist sympathizers – with justification, in certain cases – that should be treated as enemies. She preached empowerment during a period when scientific management sought to take the skills and autonomy away from working people.

Parker Follett also anticipated thinking on leadership. She argued that dictatorial methods are ineffective in the workplace, and that true leaders inspire people to achieve of their best. Leadership should not mean coercion but rather the opposite: "The greatest service the teacher can render the student is to increase his freedom – his free range of activity and thought and his power of control."[3]

The current moves towards partnership between senior managers and staff, and towards leadership by example and encouraging commitment, are perfectly in line with this philosophy. A near exact replica of such thinking can be found in the contemporary teaching of Henry Mintzberg, among others (see "People move center-stage," Chapter 6), but Parker Follett's was a message that was starkly out of kilter with the political and managerial theories that were dominant at the time. One of the few similar developments of the day was the establishment in the UK of the Industrial Society, dedicated to the principle of partnership and learning in the workplace in the 1920s.

EMPLOYMENT RIGHTS AND THE LAW

To a large extent, ordinary employees turned to trade unions or to political reform to improve welfare at work. Extreme policies of laissez-faire and minimal state protection from unemployment ended with the great Depression in the 1930s.

These developments included the USA, in spite of its reputation (held largely outside the country, and particularly in mainland Europe) as being a haven of cut-throat capitalism. President's Roosevelt's New Deal reforms in the 1930s included a national minimum wage and trade union recognition, which survived a partial return to deregulation under President Reagan in the 1980s. Moreover, the New Deal was accepted and in some cases enthusiastically endorsed by leading industrialists.[4] Protection against discrimination on the grounds of race was introduced and strengthened between 1964 and the end of the century. Anti-discrimination legislation covering women began with the Equal Pay Act of 1963, and was extended to disabled people in 1991. Generally, however, employment protection remained weak in developing countries.

Legislation, in some cases followed by expensive lawsuits, has paved the way for equal rights to employment and to promotion for people from ethnic minorities. It is only recently that the encouragement of diversity has been seen as having business benefits in itself, by opening up new routes to customers from different ethnic groups (this is discussed further in Chapter 5 and in *Managing Diversity*).

Other countries have well-developed collective rights in law. Most Continental European nations have compulsory employee consultation laws covering industrial restructurings. At the time of writing (summer 2001) the European Union had just agreed a binding law for all 15 member countries, guaranteeing such a right in workplaces with more than 50 employees. French companies must submit an annual *bilan social*, giving details of welfare, entitlements, and opportunities for employees. In the UK, Margaret Thatcher repealed wage protection and trade union rights legislation in the 1980s, but these reforms were partially reversed at the end of the 1990s by the Labour Government, which also signed up to European Union labor protection laws.

PSYCHOLOGICAL THEORIES

Charting a separate path, largely in academe, was the rise of the "human relations" school of management thinking, particularly focused on motivation. The seminal work was the research at the Western Electric factory in Hawthorne, Illinois, USA, begun in 1926 by psychologist Elton Mayo with the help of generous funding from the Rockefeller Foundation. It made the discovery that improvements in physical conditions to groups of workers had a negligible effect on productivity, and that significant improvements appeared to be derived from intangible matters such as the way in which people were treated.

This sparked an industry of psychological studies on motivation and groupwork. In 1954 Abraham Maslow published his celebrated hierarchy of human motivational needs, while in 1960 Douglas McGregor published *The Human Side of Enterprise*, which put forward Theory X and Theory Y. This proposed that managers tended to treat employees as conscripts who needed incentives and coercion (Theory X); or that they were free agents needing a sense of purpose (Theory Y). Later psychological work developed theories of human drives, such as achievement, and of personality types (these developments are discussed in greater detail in *Motivation Express*).

The post-war years also saw a rapid growth in attempts at essaying a scientific approach towards intelligence, aptitude, and selection. Groundwork had been laid by the psychologists Alfred Binet and William Stern, the latter producing the famous Intelligence Quotient, or IQ.

Assessment centers began in the Second World War, where they were developed simultaneously by the US, German, and British armed forces as a means of selecting officers for promotion. The British Civil Service was the first non-military organization to use such a center, while US telecoms giant AT&T established one in 1956. In the centers, candidates for jobs spend a day or more undergoing a range of personality, aptitude, and intelligence tests. By the early 1970s these had become commonplace and renamed assessment and development centers, as they took on responsibilities for development of existing staff as well as for recruitment (these developments are charted in *Recruitment and Retention Express*).

JAPANESE AND GERMAN MANUFACTURERS DEVELOP PARTNERSHIP

The post-war years saw the continued rise and consolidation of the large corporation, with its specialist departments and strong hierarchy. In most of the capitalist world during the Cold War personnel management did become established, but clearly as a junior discipline, administering pay, benefits, disciplinary procedures and offering a welfare service that became known patronizingly as "tea and sympathy." General management did not concern itself too much with personnel matters, as business success was deemed to come from operational efficiencies, the best technology, and the correct strategy. The pioneering work on assessment and motivation, described above, had little direct influence on senior management practice.

Some countries departed from this rigid demarcation, however. French companies placed a strong emphasis on training and, with engineering disciplines enjoying the same status as the more traditional professions, its manufacturers developed strongly.

The most radical departures in terms of human resources management came in the two principal losers of the Second World War, Japan and Germany, both of which established managerial practices based on employee involvement and partnership, which were anathema to most of the West, particularly the English-speaking countries. There were differences between the two approaches, however, and they require separate discussion.

Japan and *hoshin kanri*

The Japanese system became known as *hoshin kanri*, which is often translated as meaning "policy deployment process," but a key feature is employee involvement. It could equally well be described as meaning "everyone is involved in strategy." Translation requires care, owing to cultural differences, with Japanese people favoring a more collective, less individualistic approach than most Western nations. The etymology of *hoshin kanri* suggests a shining light on the compass designed to illuminate the way for all ships of a fleet. As such, it is understood to embrace teamwork and cooperation, rather than quality as arising from edicts announced from the top management.[5]

In 1950 a North American statistician called W. Edwards Deming addressed the Japanese Union of Scientists and Engineers for the first time, as part of a concerted effort by the US authorities to bolster capitalism in the country in the face of the strength of Communism in the region. It was the start of a series of lectures and seminars that, with hindsight, can be seen to be as influential as any event in the history of management.

Deming's philosophy was different from that of most Western management thinkers. He may have shared the objectives of the early practitioners of scientific management – elimination of waste, quality control, and high efficiency – but his method was an inversion of Taylorism: such objectives can only be achieved by trusting people, not removing their autonomy, he argued. He had come to the conclusion that fear in the hearts of employees was the biggest enemy of high standards. Other touring lecturers, such as Joseph Juran and Homer Sarasohn, brought a similar message.

This approach found a willing audience in Japan, where it suited the country's collective culture as it was more attuned to the notions of teamworking than the more traditional, individualistic Western approach. The practice of job rotation produced senior executives with a rounded view of the business. It is not uncommon for the president of a Japanese firm to have been responsible for training and personnel at some stage in his development; until very recently this was unheard of in the West[6] (see Komatsu case study, Chapter 7).

Within a few decades Japanese manufacturers had become the most successful in the world, and at the heart of their approach was personnel management. When the power of Japanese manufacturing was at its peak, in the 1980s, attempts were made to introduce the underlying principles to Western companies, with varying degrees of success. Deming became popular and, in 1986, he published *Out of the Crisis*, setting out his 14 principles of management. Even though eight of these principles concerned employee motivation, the idea of Total Quality was still, in the view of some, implemented in a rather mechanistic way, rather than by way of a deep-rooted cultural change.[7]

A more thoroughgoing approach to implementing Japanese approaches in other cultures was set out in the 1981 work *Theory Z: How American Business Can Meet the Japanese Challenge*, written by William Ouchi. It appeared at a time when there was a crisis of confidence in Western corporations. He defined the key principles as:

» lifetime employment;
» job rotation;
» shared information;
» collective decision-making; and
» quality emphasis.

The last four of these have been implemented to a greater or lesser degree in the subsequent two decades outside Japan, while employers have marched in an opposite direction with respect to the first. The underlying reasons for this will be discussed in Chapter 6.

Germany and works councils

It was North Americans who kick-started the business partnership pattern in Japan that would one day undermine their own corporations. With similar irony it was the British who assisted Germany's industrial revival. After the Second World War Britain had a security interest in promoting Germany's democracy, and to put in checks and balances on German businesses to make it more difficult for them to support a dictator, as they had in the 1930s. It was British advisors who helped set up the employer–employee business partnership arrangements in post-war West Germany, giving unions a say in the running of enterprises that their British counterparts never enjoyed themselves.

The approach was known as *Mitbestimmung* – participation in decision-making – and its cornerstone was the *Betriebsrat*, the works council, which gives employee representatives a say in key decisions, including those covering working hours, vacations, personnel policy, work organizations, criteria for job evaluation, and vocational training. The process undoubtedly makes decision-making slower than in less-regulated workplaces, but arguably more effective. In the 1970s the German motor industry avoided strike action that crippled counterparts in Anglo-Saxon nations, and it developed multi-skilled teamworking that helped dramatic rises in productivity.

One striking factor about the German and Japanese systems, however, is that they were not dominant forever. Both ran into difficulties in the 1990s, although the better companies from each country, such as Sony, Toyota, and Volkswagen, remain far ahead of most of their competitors. The difficulties of the Japanese concept of lifetime employment are discussed further in Chapter 6.

Nonetheless, both *hoshin kanri* and *Mitbestimmung* appear rather formulaic and bureaucratic to those familiar with the new economy. It could be that they are simply more suited to heavy engineering, with its need for long-term planning and sophisticated project management and labor relations, than for intellectual property or customer-service companies. Certainly in Germany smaller, new economy companies are ditching the works councils and involving their staff through US-style stock options.[8] Works councils are not compulsory unless employees or unions demand one. Despite this, in 2001 the government of Gerhard Schröder increased the influence of the *Betriebsrat*, giving it a say on environmental issues and job security, and greater control over training. Another problem with the *Betriebsrat* is that, by taking over some of the traditional responsibilities of the personnel department, it has possibly held up the development of the personnel profession in Germany.

Japan and West Germany exerted some influence on their near neighbors, though the US model carried some weight also. In the US-influenced world the profile and philosophy of people management went through profound changes, which were not consistently in the same direction.

The 1980s saw the introduction of the term "human resources." This could be interpreted in one of two ways. Calling employees resources could be seen as progressive, recognizing that they are assets to the company; on the other hand, the term is inanimate and can be employed by disciples of scientific management who see people as cogs in the wheel. Its use became associated with the great management fad of the early 1990s, business process re-engineering, which used a mechanistic metaphor and was widely perceived to have failed. Even the architects of the approach, Michael Hammer and James Champy, admitted that they had "forgotten the people element."[9] The basis for the original supposition that companies do not comprise people was not made clear.

The failures of re-engineering, together with similar rates of failure for mergers and other restructurings,[10] have revealed that employees cannot be told what to do; at least not without a pay-off. Until the 1990s obedience could be purchased by the promise of employment security, but this was deliberately taken away during the downsizing and restructuring exercises. Managers discovered that they could not achieve flexible working, commitment, teamworking, and continual learning without the cooperation of employees, and falling unemployment heightened this need.

Intangible capital overtook tangible assets in 1992, as the world economy entered a new phase, dubbed either the information revolution or the new economy. Knowledge and skills became more important to competitive advantage than access to capital or commodities. *The Learning Organization*, written by Peter Senge and published in 1990, received less fanfare than *Re-Engineering the Corporation* (Hammer and Champy), but it has had a more lasting impact, as companies perceive that their collective abilities, rather than their lean processes, are key – though of course many firms have sought to emphasize both.

The most recent fad, emotional intelligence, is very different. Since the publication of the book of the same name in 1996 (written by Daniel Goleman) it has become respectable, even mandatory, for managers to talk about motivating and empowering people. This means that the difference between the US model and the German and Japanese approaches has lessened, as North American businesses learn from the mistakes of excessive downsizing in the early 1990s. All influential management thinkers now sing a similar chorus about leadership by inspiration, rather than by instruction; and of the importance of engaging and communicating with the workforce, although this approach may not survive unscathed from the renewed redundancies that have occurred in 2001. This is discussed further in Chapter 6.

TIMELINE

» **1799**: Robert Owen buys New Lanark and sets up his "model" village.
» **1867**: Karl Marx publishes *Das Kapital*.
» **1911**: Frederick Taylor publishes *The Principles of Scientific Management*, heralding piece-rates and the moving assembly line.
» **1914**: Henry Ford is forced to double pay rates to $5 a day in order to reduce labor turnover on the assembly line.
» **1922**: The Industrial Society is set up in the UK to educate and campaign for partnership in the workplace.

» **1924**: Mary Parker Follett publishes *Creative Experience*.
» **1926**: The Hawthorne Experiments begin.
» **1929**: Wall Street Crash heralds the end of laissez-faire capitalism in developed economies.
» **1933**: President Roosevelt unveils the New Deal.
» **1940s**: Assessment centers for officers pioneered by armed forces engaged in the Second World War.
» **1950**: W. Edwards Deming addresses the Japanese Union of Scientists and Engineers, telling them that employees must be involved in efforts to improve productivity.
» **1956**: AT&T sets up assessment center.
» **1960**: Japanese firms begin quality circles.
» **1964**: Civil Rights Act prohibits discrimination based on race, color, religion, sex, or national origin in US organizations.
» **Mid 1970s**: The term "human resources" enters management vocabulary.
» **1980**: Hiroyuki Itami publishes *Mobilizing Invisible Assets*. Unemployment starts to soar in the West, caused by recession and weakness against Japanese competition.
» **1986**: Deming publishes *Out of the Crisis*.
» **1990**: Peter Senge publishes *The Learning Organization*.
» **1992**: Intangible capital surpasses tangible capital in US firms.
» **1994**: Swedish insurance group Skandia publishes intellectual capital report.
» **1996**: Daniel Goleman publishes *Emotional Intelligence*.
» **2000**: War for talent reaches fever pitch in USA as unemployment falls below 4 percent.
» **2001**: Technology firms start laying off staff as downturn bites.

KEY LEARNING POINTS

» Early phase of industrialization led to de-skilling; reinforced by scientific management.
» Management thinker Mary Parker Follett was alone in advocating employee–employer partnership in early twentieth century.

» Employees sought improved welfare through the law and trade unions, rather than from the employer.

» Statutory protection began in a major way in the 1930s, in the aftermath of the Wall Street Crash of 1929.

» The "human relations" school of motivational studies began with the Hawthorne experiments in the 1920s, which found that styles of management, rather than working environment, held the key to better productivity.

» Personnel became confined to a separate department in the post-war years, with the exception of Japan and Germany, which fostered integration of employee development and general management.

» Principles of scientific management re-emerged strongly with the advent of business process re-engineering in late 1980s, though this was later perceived to have failed.

» Intangible capital overtook tangible capital in 1992, since when management of people has become more central; paradoxically, Japanese and German models hit problems.

NOTES

1 Thompson, E.P. (1968) *The Making of the English Working Class*. Pelican.

2 Parker Follett, M. (1940) *Dynamic Administration*. Harper Bros, New York.

3 Parker Follett, M. (1940) *Dynamic Administration*. Harper Bros, New York.

4 Crainer, S. (2000) *The Management Century*. Booz-Allen & Hamilton.

5 Witcher, B. *et al.* (1997) *The Hoshin Kanri Method: A Position Paper*. University of East Anglia; and Akao, Y. (ed.) (1991) *Hoshin Kanri: Policy Deployment for Successful TQM* (originally published as *Hoshin kanri katsuyo no jissai*, 1988). Productivity Press, Cambridge MA.

6 See *Global HR*, July/August (2001) Reed Business Information.

7 Morton, C. (1994) *Becoming World Class*. Macmillan Business, London.

8 Bryson, A. (2000) "Who's afraid of German labor law?" *Frankfurter Allgemeine*, November 21.

9 Fast Company, *The Fad that Forgot People*, Fast Company, www. fastcompany.com/online/01/reengin.html.

10 KPMG (1998) *Mergers and Acquisitions: Unlocking Shareholder Value: The Keys to Success*. KPMG.

The E-Dimension of People Management

» People management was largely untouched by technology until the late 1990s, since when it has begun transforming approaches, particularly to recruitment and training.
» Outsourcing is much easier and continues apace, but presents formidable challenges of accountability.
» Automation frees personnel managers to help business more.
» New economy start-ups have not followed a consistent approach to people management; much has depended upon the personality of the founders.
» Case study: IBM Europe.

"Any sufficiently advanced technology is indistinguishable from magic."

Arthur C. Clarke

Automation has come late to personnel systems, especially when one draws a contrast with the robotics that have powered motor-manufacturing since the late 1970s, but it has arrived in a big way. The spread of the Internet, and equally significantly of intranets, since the mid 1990s has enabled companies to replace all or most routine personnel administration with self-entry data-recording systems that are updated in real time. Members of staff enter such things as their own personal details, their CVs when applying, and the training courses attended and those requested.

Technology affects people management in other ways. It offers new forms of instant communication, enabling transnational teams to share product and customer knowledge more quickly and more fully. It has resulted in flatter hierarchies by reducing the number of people devoted to purely administrative tasks, increasing the teamworking skills needed by employees and the human resources specialists who may support them (see also *Teamworking Express*). It has also brought personnel management to the fore by creating an extra demand for programmers, causing some companies to be affected by endemic skills shortages, even as redundancy programs are announced.

AUTOMATION OF THE NUTS AND BOLTS

The transfer of most personnel administration from paper to intranets and the Internet removes much processing of paper from the tasks of the conventional personnel department. Logistically the operation is handled most efficiently from a single service center serving several units, with staff geared more towards handling queries from staff by phone or e-mail as the technology takes the strain of the data processing. This in turn makes the service ripe for outsourcing, and oil giant BP-Amoco blazed a trail by announcing a link-up with California-based Exult in 1999 to handle all routine personnel bureaucracy. Other multinationals, such as IBM and Procter & Gamble, have retained ownership of the service center, though from the technological point of view the set-up is similar.

Whether in-sourced or outsourced, companies have found that they can install a single, standardized system for personnel systems, although differing data protection laws in different countries qualify the extent to which it can be completely uniform. Such laws are particularly strong in the European Union, the 15 countries of which have a single Act that prohibits the re-use of most personal data without the prior consent of the individual. It also covers many paper records and puts limits on the use of automatic "sifting" of CVs when processing applications.

The spread of technology has a significant impact for people in personnel departments. Routine administrative jobs are disappearing, but others are emerging, though not necessarily at the same rate. Generally the new posts will be more outward-focused, based on communicating directly with employees and advising line managers; they may also include language skills (see IBM case study at the end of this chapter). A personnel professional who, in the early 1990s, would have been responsible for ensuring that the application forms were up to date and compliant with a new law, and who would give advice when asked, would now be expected to work closely with line managers to learn about the skills needed for a team, and what the best recruitment Websites are. Alternatively he or she may be working in the call center for a multinational corporation, having learned a new language, and be giving advice on recruitment to line managers across a continent.

A lower headcount for the administrative task does not diminish its importance. David Ulrich, one of the foremost thinkers and authors in human resources management, divides the principal disciplines of the personnel profession into four: strategic partner, employee champion, change agent, and administrator (see Chapter 8). The administrator is of equal importance, he argues, and he deploys the following fictitious situation to demonstrate his case:

"The four managers were arguing their relative importance. The strategic partner said it was obvious that she was the most important, as she advised the board on the relevance of the HR approach to the fundamental positioning of the organization. The change agent countered that organizations are continually evolving in rapid markets so that he was the most important, while the employee champion pointed out how employee relations tended to make or break any organization. Then the administrator said: 'Right, none of you are getting paid next month.'"

What is clear, though, is that those specialising in administration need to be technically aware, and may well be promoted from the IT side, rather than from a background in personnel. Such an awareness of technology is of increasing importance to all human resources professionals. Concetta Lanciaux, executive vice-president of France-based luxury goods group LVMH, predicts that those with a combination of expertise in IT systems and people management will come to dominate the profession:

> "This is a very big area; ten years from now these are the people who will be running the HR function. It used to be psychologists and legal people or those with a general business background. In the future it could be engineers who got into HR or HR people who are at ease with the technology."[1]

There are potential benefits of these developments in terms of employee relations, but there are also potential pitfalls.

E-COMMUNICATION AND RECRUITMENT

Speed and ease of communication ought to facilitate the sharing of business goals, although there are difficulties bound up in the problems of information overload through excessive use of e-mails, with some people receiving over 100 each day. More fundamentally, intra-business communication can only be as effective as the organizational commitment to the principle. The first instinct of many executives is still to keep only themselves privy to important information and this habit is not of itself altered by any change in technology. Some employers use the technology to keep close tabs on employees, which could weaken trust. This is explored further in *Motivation Express*.

Nonetheless, the speed and convenience of communication has undoubtedly helped organizations spread globally. The need to communicate frequently is often shared by people of the same discipline, who may be spread around the world; Internet chat-rooms, e-mails and video-conferencing can greatly expand the quality as well as the quantity of interchange (see case study, Chapter 5).

Telecoms companies such as Cisco and Nortel, before the downturn in 2001, became ever more innovative in aggressive and often surreptitious hiring techniques in a war for talent. Techniques involved tracing a browser on the company's "situations vacant" Web page and inviting them for interview, and tracking software engineers who have set up their own Websites. Such approaches will not become un-invented because these groups have made redundancies in 2001. Skills shortages are likely to remain an issue in the technology area, an issue that has prompted some richer countries to reduce immigration barriers (see Chapter 5).

Even personality tests can go online. The international test provider SHL, for example, can offer its tests on behalf of a recruiter via the latter's HR Website. The client company sends an e-mail to the candidate with a password, the candidate then completes the questionnaire, and SHL sends the results to the potential employer.

THE PITFALLS

There are concerns, however, in creating virtual relationships, particularly where a third-party outsource provider is dealing with sensitive matters such as personnel. Some companies draw a distinction between administrative tasks that are more suited to automation and outsourcing, and more developmental areas, such as training on interpersonal skills.

The application form for promotion can be put online and administered by a third party, but this may not be the right move for the management development training that accompanies the application. Similarly, the Microsoft Excel course can easily be done on the Internet, but the individual's appraisal will need to include at least some face-to-face contact.

A UK survey of personnel professionals carried out in 2001 by Oxford psychologists Press (a supplier of psychometric tests) and the journal *People Management*, found that two-thirds of respondents had reservations about using online personality tests at the recruitment stage. The principal concerns were over lack of control: whether the candidates had understood the instructions properly, and difficulties in verifying who had completed the form.[2]

The trick with application of e-solutions in personnel is to ensure that it is the management, and not the technology, that is in charge, and that culturally sensitive matters stay firmly in-house. Ian Mann, chief executive of HR consultancy ECA International, comments: "Five years ago outsourcing was the thing, but everyone is in-sourcing now and are re-recruiting [to their personnel departments]. It is about people. When you outsource you are giving away some control, no matter how much you seek to retain this through contracts, and big corporations want more control, especially if they are going into recession." Switching administration to a third party can have a particularly unsettling effect on expatriates, he adds, who already have a tendency to feel paranoid, or at best part-removed from the rest of the organization:

> "If you outsource you are telling expatriates, 'We want you on board but do not bother talking to us.' Where the service is completely mechanistic, like payroll, that is one thing, but if you are outsourcing a policy issue you cannot legislate for every eventuality. Managers have to interpret principles. If it is handled by a third party then HR gets blamed by the management for something that goes wrong, HR blames the provider and you have a pass-the-buck culture."

Freedom from bureaucracy that the Internet offers should help personnel professionals to be more closely involved in the business, learning more about the job descriptions and conditions of the places for which they are recruiting, and of the people whose training and development they are charged with encouraging. This, however, is an opportunity, not a given. Companies need to use the freedom, and to apply technological solutions where it is right for the business, rather than where it is straightforward logistically.

Randall Schuler and Susan Jackson, professors of human resources at Rutgers University, comment:

> "Learning organizations [must] invest in creating face-to-face opportunities for learning and knowledge sharing as well as information technologies. Meetings around the water cooler are encouraged rather than discouraged. Social events, mentoring, classroom-based workshops, conferences and community service are all seen as forums for implicit knowledge sharing and learning."[3]

While social events remain integral to many personnel functions, technology can open up access and encourage participation at the initial stage. This is particularly the case in training, which has at times suffered from a "dowdy" image, but can appear more cutting-edge and dynamic when presented online. Many individuals, particularly executives, have neglected their own development and feel that they do not have time to go on a three-day course. If, however, a personally tailored training program can be relayed to them at least partly via the Internet, to be studied in their own time in a few hours, and linked clearly with a path to promotion, the prospect becomes enticing. US industrial group Parker Hannifin has discovered this in its application of training technology, in partnership with third-party supplier skillsoft.com (see Chapter 5 for case study; see also *Online People Processes*, and *Training Express*).

DOTCOMS AND THE NEW ECONOMY

A new culture has accompanied the spread of e-technology, with a natural impact on people management. First-name terms, casual dress, and informal boss-to-worker relationships have been features of the new economy and have left a seemingly permanent mark, in spite of the temporary nature of the dotcom investment boom and bust between 1998 and 2001. Not all dotcoms have failed and, in any case, the development towards a less formal culture predates the dotcom craze, having been a feature of such service-sector companies as Virgin and Ben & Jerry's Ice Cream.

There has been no consistent pattern in terms of development of people and integration of people management to the business in newer start-ups. Formal human resources departments have not been popular, and have been introduced only when the size of the organization became such that it was indispensable, and the personnel policy has depended largely upon the personalities of the founders. As such it can be very positive, quite negative, or mixed.

The online bookseller Amazon.com has faced strong criticism from unions in the US and Europe for failing to recognize trade unions and for imposing allegedly strict rules on junior staff for the numbers of packages to be packed per minute, in the style of an old-fashioned "Taylorist" factory. The company has defended itself, arguing that every employee is regarded as an associate, that pay is above average, and that it offers share options and opportunities for self-advancement.[4]

SUMMARY

By definition, new technology will not stay new; but, by the same token, new systems will appear and media that have had an uncertain start, such as WAP technology, could reappear in a more effective form. The Internet, by transforming personnel administration and internal means of communication, has brought about multiple direct and indirect effects upon companies' people management systems and approaches.

What has also become clear is that basic principles of management, such as trust, integrity, and strategic thinking, do not change. Technology will not of itself train workers, promote understanding, foster morale, solve employee relations problems, or find the ideal candidate. Companies have to exercise judgment on how to apply technology, while staying abreast of other aspects of the new economy, which are globalization and the rise of intangible assets. These matters will be discussed in the following chapters.

BEST PRACTICE
IBM

Routine administration in personnel departments can be cut by two-thirds with the use of new technology, global IT giant IBM has found. At its European human resources service center in Portsmouth, southern UK, it has cut costs by 10 percent, year on year, between 1995 and 2001.

Up to 80 percent of inquiries to the HR department of IBM are handled by the intranet or by a call center service. HR people – from specialists to quite junior administrative and call center staff – can now expect to be working in separate international HR units. The HR department reckons it is in a transition, moving from spending around 60 percent of its time on routine queries to just 20 percent, with the bulk of activity focused either on implementing particular programs, or dealing with strategy.

In switching from country-specific HR approaches, the company found that only 20 percent of the processes were determined by national systems, such as tax arrangements. The rest could be put on a common platform, eliminating a huge amount of duplication.

Backing from the top of the organization has helped, said Stephanie Voquer, director of human resources for IBM Global Services. In the 1999 annual report the chairman Lou Gerstner wrote that training, development, and knowledge management were going to be high priorities for the group. "We felt that we had endorsement," said Voquer. Distinguishing between administration and strategy helps the strategic input. In particular, the HR function has responsibility for developing top managers. Voquer went on to say, "This has been crucial, because leaders before were not successful. These were not the ones that were going to take us forward. We have looked at the experience that made successful leaders, rather than the fixed positions; we have looked at the type of skills and the type of leadership development that we can count on for the future."

The strategic part of the personnel function is sufficiently freed to be able to offer one-on-one support to executives. Specialisms within the department are divided broadly into four: HR partners, offering close support to executives; experts on the full range of subjects; administration employees; and those working in the service center. IBM Europe has opted for a real service center, rather than a virtual one, and it is located in Portsmouth.

"Also, from the HR people there was fear that their jobs were going to be threatened. Initially they did not see that opportunities would be created," said Voquer. In early 2001 the HR department was told of a further 10 percent cut in its budget. "Before, we would have been devastated. Now we say 'What is the best way to deliver this?'" Voquer added.

KEY LEARNING POINTS

» Automation has spread rapidly to personnel systems, and feature self-entry personal data systems and online learning and testing. Outsourcing has also featured.

» Internet and intranet systems have helped international employee communication.

» New opportunities for delivery of personnel services have arisen through e-technology, particularly in recruitment and training, but the "personal touch" is seen as essential for many functions.

» Technology can overcome a "dowdy" image for training.

» Pitfalls with new technology applications concern questions of control and lines of responsibility. Outsourcing can compound the difficulties.

» New economy companies have not followed any set pattern of integration of people management and strategy.

» Successful applications feature strong management that applies technology in the interests of the business, rather than be guided by logistical simplicity.

NOTES

1 See *Global HR*, September 2001, Reed Business Information.

2 See www.peoplemanagement.co.uk/psymetrics/results.html.

3 Schuler, R. and Jackson, S. (2001) "Turning knowledge into business advantage," *Financial Times*, January 15.

4 Maguire, K. (2001) "UK workforce attacks Amazon," *Guardian*, April 14 (www.guardian.co.uk/Archive/Article/0,4273,4170 417,00. html).

The Global Dimension of People Management

» The global economy increasingly resembles prosperous, knowledge-rich regions, rather than rich and poor countries.
» There is tension between local and colonial-style management in multinationals. Some opt for a tight–loose structure; more than one approach can be successful.
» Cross-cultural working can be beneficial to global companies.
» The contribution of employees is more transparent in expatriate placements.
» Questions of asylum, mobility, and work permits reveal clashing interests in the global economy.
» Case study: Parker Hannifin.

"People are not afraid of change, they are afraid of uncertainty."
Juan Somavia, director general of the International Labor
Organization, at a conference on the Future of Work,
Employment and Social Protection (Annecy, south-east France,
January 2001)

NEW OPPORTUNITIES

Although anti-poverty protestors gather outside every trade, political and economic meeting involving wealthy vested interests to complain about globalization, the breaking down of trade barriers has offered opportunities for developing countries, as well as for multinationals. Research and IT agencies in India, for example, sell their services directly over the Internet, without any import tariffs or quotas that apply to agriculture or commodities – traditionally the staple exports of developing countries.

Increasingly this illustrates how the divisions in the world economy are between "knowledge-rich" people and business clusters, and those groups of people that lack relevant skills, rather than between nations. So the Bangalore IT cluster is becoming more prosperous not only relative to nearby agricultural villages in India, but also to many industrial towns in North America and northern Europe. Will Hutton, chief executive of the Industrial Society in the UK, describes these as "hot" and "cold" networks, exhibiting respectively virtuous and vicious circles of development and learning or, conversely, lack of education and unemployment. Hutton points out that they can exist just a few hundred yards from each other in cities like New York and London.

This pattern was comprehensively identified by Michael Porter in *The Competitive Advantage of Nations* (1990), who pointed out that supposed disadvantages, such as high labor costs in some countries, are outweighed by skills, particularly specialist clusters of skills, such as the Japanese motor manufacturers, Californian software developers, and so on. It can also be witnessed in smaller, niche industries, such as Italian ski-boot manufacturers or British biscuit-makers (see also Chapter 6, "People move center-stage"). It is the human resource that determines the wealth of regions and nations – and of international companies.

MULTINATIONALS AND THE LOCAL VERSUS GLOBAL DILEMMA

There are parallel developments in multinational companies, many of which resemble clusters of geographically dispersed businesses, rather than a single corporation. New technology can aid this development: as fewer people can be needed to sustain business in a region than before, quite small companies can have a global reach, while larger firms can set up Internet chat rooms and other facilities to enable people to discuss problems and learn from one another (see Chapter 4).

Companies are often seeking the "tight–loose" balancing act, described by management thinkers Tom Peters and Robert Waterman,[1] in which they seek to maximise local autonomy but maintain a strong ethos or culture (see the Parker Hannifin case study at end of this chapter, and see also *Teamworking Express*). Global companies want to retain the integrity of the brand and ensure that customer experience is broadly the same throughout the world, but not bind the actions of regional managers too tightly. This can be particularly important to maintain, but particularly difficult in practice, following a cross-border merger. Which culture of the two firms will predominate? Or will there be a new one?[2]

Hence, while there have been moves in recent years for multinational companies to decentralize and to switch away from the so-called "colonial" structures, with control held tightly in the central office and key positions abroad filled by seconded expatriate staff, there are also initiatives to spread and maintain a single culture. Hiring and training of local staff, and inculcating them in the company's culture, is a priority for many. In the 1980s Motorola engaged in long-term scenario planning in the newly opened market of China to set its strategy, and established a corporate university in Beijing at a time when such a move was unfashionable. It promised no "glass ceiling" for locally recruited and promoted Chinese nationals who graduated from the establishment. Staff retention has been significantly better in Motorola than in other inward investors in China.[3] This appears to square the circle of being global and local simultaneously, but it requires unchanging commitment and long-term planning. Such heavy investment will not be appropriate in every nation or for every company.

More than one approach can be effective, however. Coca-Cola, for example, retains many controls at its headquarters in Atlanta, Georgia, while the oil giant BP fosters more international mobility, coping with the formidable administrative challenge of recruiting from, and appointing to, a total of 70 countries, each with its own tax and legal system, amounting to a maximum possible 4,900 permutations in arranging employment contracts.

Some use of expatriates will always remain. If the objective is transfer of skills then, by definition, this involves use of expatriates from the country with the desired skills to the region that has a need for them. Similarly, many multinational companies want their managers who are being groomed for senior positions to have international experience, so sometimes executives are sent to another country largely for the experience.

Divergence in living standards remains a powerful disincentive to mobility, according to the cost of living survey carried out by international HR consultancy ECA (see www.eca-international.com). For example, to take two affluent countries in Europe, Switzerland and Finland, it is better to live in Switzerland than Finland by a factor of two to three times in terms of purchasing power. If the company has a policy of paying local rates then going from Switzerland to Finland is highly problematic.

Diversity

The benefits of a diverse workforce are beginning to be appreciated by companies. In the example of Motorola in China there is an obvious advantage in having people trained to the same level as Motorola specialists in North America, who also know the Chinese market and culture. On the other hand, in the case of Coca-Cola or, say, Cadillac cars, the firm is selling a US icon, and it is probably more effective to have a real American selling the product than a local person.

But diversity helps in other ways. There are clear cultural differences in the way people approach managerial and other dilemmas, and being able to deploy more than one can raise the effectiveness of a team. Anglo-Saxons, for example, are good at categorizing, while many Asian peoples are better at seeing the big picture. A consultancy industry has grown up in recent years to educate top businesses on the subtleties and range of these cultural differences, and how to make use of them and avoid damaging disputes that have a cultural clash at their root. Probably the most influential work in this regard is *Riding the Waves of Culture – Understanding Cultural Diversity in Business*, written by Fons Trompenaars and Charles Hampden-Turner and published in 1997 (2nd edn). Such work is also applicable for smaller companies operating in just one country that is multi-racial. Together with other consultants, Trompenaars and Hampden-Turner advise companies on teamworking. This issue is explored in more depth in *Motivation Express*.

Transparency of people's contributions in the global firm

Human resources matters are closer to the top of the agenda in international placements than in many areas of business. One reason concerns the barriers to managerial mobility posed by personal reasons – for instance, the desire for an increasing number of the spouses of expatriate managers to have their own career, or the educational needs of children. Such employees are often very valuable to the company, so there is a more than usually clear link between the "soft" issues of employee welfare and business performance.

The issues can be intricate. Singaporean parents, for example, are particularly keen for their children's upbringing to be uninterrupted. In the Singaporean national curriculum every child is expected to attain a certain level in English and Mandarin Chinese; such instruction cannot be guaranteed elsewhere in the world, so a child missing a few years could be set back considerably when he or she returns.

Traditionally children of expatriate staff would be educated in boarding schools, and the free provision of such education was a perk for people to work abroad. Social changes have seen boarding schools go out of fashion, however, as parents want to have more contact with their children.

The development of the international baccalaureate may alleviate this situation. There are now dozens of schools around the world that operate the curriculum devised by the Geneva-based International Baccalaureate Organization.

The other factor driving personnel matters up the international management agenda is that the cost and the value of people on an expatriate placement, or of running a fairly small regional office, are highly visible. A single person or small team can be responsible for sales across several countries, and their contacts and knowledge can be worth millions to the company, so it is simply good management to ensure that such individuals have all their needs catered for. The loss of just one can be costly for the company.

The human resources consultancy Traqs has developed a tool for gauging the value of a placement. It does not put monetary value on the worth of an individual, but produces a relative "score" of the worth of a placement to the individual, to the host country and to the home country. This avoidance of a financial figure is in keeping with measures of intellectual capital (see Chapter 6). The Traqs method scores the merits of an individual out of ten on various attributes, and makes a similar assessment on the difficulties of the task and the relevance of the skills to the task. The questionnaires involved also tease out the likelihood of the person actually wanting to do the job – this is important, as the risk of someone quitting must be taken into account in planning and in setting the salary.

The scores are fed into a model, which places the individual on a grid showing the relative benefits of a placement to the parties involved – the home company, the host company, and the employee. A highly skilled specialist sent to trouble-shoot in a part of the world that she does not want to go to will benefit the host country far more than the other stakeholders. By contrast, if the host takes on a recent graduate for work experience as part of a management development program, the interests are inverted. The Traqs calculation helps set the package that would be needed.[4]

Asylum, mobility and work permits

The US President George W. Bush's agreement with President Vicente Fox of Mexico in February 2001, to agree a guest worker program, marked a turning point in international mobility. The steady drop of US unemployment to under 4 percent at the end of the long 1990s boom meant that the world's largest economy was running out of people and a long history of strict immigration controls came to an end. In October 2000 the US Congress had increased the annual cap on the number of skilled-worker visas from 115,000 to 195,000.

Rival plans on the guest worker scheme put forward in the US Senate have differed over whether temporary employees – who are wanted by employers in the agriculture, construction and service industries – would have the right to apply for US citizenship. Civil rights groups say failure to grant citizens' rights would place immigrant employees in the ambiguous position of *Gastarbeiters* in Germany, who are permanent residents without political rights.

Also in 2001, 20 of the top multinational companies, including Shell, Siemens, UBS Warburg, and Unilever, joined forces to establish the pressure group Permits, to campaign for more employment rights for the spouses of expatriate staff. In the USA it has received backing from congressmen and senators and a Bill was due to be presented in 2001 proposing work permits for spouses under certain conditions. The group argues that in countries where spouses can work, including the UK, Australia and Argentina, the effect on local labour markets is negligible and the transfer of skills can be positive.

In May 2001 the Economic and Social Affairs Committee of the EU reported that Hungary had made "considerable progress" regarding freedom of movement, though it noted the potential for upheavals in labor markets given the considerably higher wages available in the West.

Whether full mobility of all people throughout the world is ever attainable is unsure, but critics of the present systems point out that mobility of capital has been assured in the capitalist world since the early 1980s, extending to other economies following the collapse of the Berlin Wall in 1989.

The economic cycle plays a major part in such developments, determining the demand in richer regions. In 2001 many large companies announced redundancy programs, and unemployment started to edge upwards in Germany, with the rate of the fall in unemployment slowing elsewhere. The Society for Human Resource Management, which is the US association for personnel managers, reported in April 2001 that the economic downturn had forced some immigrant skilled staff to return home from Silicon Valley. It says that just six months after the near doubling of the number of entry visas for technology people, many of them have been "sitting idle for months or even going back home." It reported cases of skilled foreign workers without work or working for just $250 a week – which is a fraction of the rates of a year earlier.

However, this may only be a hiatus in the move towards greater mobility of skilled workers in the global knowledge economy. The increasing relative value to an employer of a skilled versus an unskilled individual, and increasing access to markets for developing countries, means that the barriers to employment are likely to concern barriers to education and training, rather than passport control.

BEST PRACTICE

Parker Hannifin

The move towards maintaining a global culture within a decentralized international company is exemplified in the human resources policy of US-based industrial group Parker Hannifin. It manufactures control and hydraulic systems, for example producing the control mechanisms for the models used in *Jurassic Park*. There are around 250 plants worldwide, most of them quite small, employing around 200–300 people.

It is very decentralized in its structure, and used to employ many generalist human resources managers. Those attached to a plant had responsibilities across the whole range of personnel matters, from record-keeping to disciplinary procedures and employee relations, and it was felt that they had become too caught up in operational matters with a short-term focus. The group is now in the transition of switching to more specialist personnel professionals in such areas as training, recruitment, performance management, and so on. These specialists are engaged to work more creatively with the business units and to encourage cross-functional working and joint learning and development among all staff, and to be involved in long-term planning. The generalists that remain are responsible for more units and are expected to be strategic in outlook.

In training, Parker Hannifin is seeking to maximize e-learning opportunities, though balanced with face-to-face training where matters are more intangible and include teamwork and the company culture. But this is not so much to save costs, says European learning and development manager Paul Everitt, but to free the time of training specialists to work more closely with line managers and teams. The aim is to encourage continual learning, rather than see training as comprising only discrete courses. "Learning happens continually; training is perceived as an event," says Everitt.

Cross-border sharing of learning experiences is encouraged, therefore. According to Everitt, "If a sales representative goes to a customer in one country, but learns that this customer has operations in other countries, we need to share that learning." To this end, Everitt and his colleagues have encouraged international networks. In 2001 there were two global exchange programs involving high-potential employees from North America and Europe; the planned next step is to set up an Internet chat room for them so that they can learn about customers, processes or marketing opportunities from each other. There is also a leadership program, under which managers can bring dilemmas to a discussion forum for debate.

The performance management process is seen as a personal development program, rather than a mechanistic ticking of boxes in a formulaic appraisal. As such, it is the responsibility of trainers, not compensation specialists. There is no direct link with pay in the performance appraisal; instead it is seen as an opportunity to discuss ambitions and learning needs, and how the desires of the individual fit in with the ambitions of the organization.

The objective underlying all these initiatives is to maximize the benefits of both decentralization and the company's global nature. Globalization is expressed through a shared culture, and by exhibiting teamwork and networking, rather than through a single monolithic structure.

KEY LEARNING POINTS

» The global economy increasingly comprises clusters of skilled people and businesses, rather than poor or rich nations.

» The pattern is similar in global companies, some of which have the structure of a constellation of businesses, rather than a single entity.

» "Colonial" models for international businesses are less common, but there is still a strong demand for expatriate staff.

» Cultural diversity can help employers sell to new markets and deploy the different strengths of different approaches to problems.

» Human resources matters are closer to the top of the agenda in international placements than elsewhere in business because of the link between personal concerns of the expatriate and business performance; and because the cost and benefit of a small team covering a large area can be transparent.

» Labor mobility across the world is increasingly in demand by business.

NOTES

1 Peters, T. and Waterman, R. (1982) *In Search of Excellence*. Harper & Row, New York.

2 Martin, P. (1999) "The national factor," *Financial Times Europe*, August 31 (www.ft.com/fteuro/q833a.htm).

3 Gratton, L. (2000) *Living Strategy*. FT/Prentice Hall, London.

4 See www.traqs.com/etf/intro.

The State of the Art of People Management

» Many management thinkers now place people development at the heart of business strategy.
» The status of people management is confused, as two strong forces – impetus for shareholder return and rise of importance of skills and teamwork – appear to be in conflict. Some organizations are finding overlapping interests.
» Many personnel managers are "addicted to HR tools."
» The Japanese model of lifetime employment has proved difficult to sustain, but this does not imply a simple return to "hire and fire."
» Labor regulation is growing but is not always a barrier to organizational success.
» Intellectual capital has challenged conventional accountancy and makes people matters more central.

"Knowing how to retain and develop human capital is a new frontier."
Giuseppe Guida, director general of Skillvest France, a human resources consultancy

PEOPLE MOVE CENTER-STAGE. OR DO THEY?

Jeffrey Pfeffer, Stanford University professor and a long-standing critic of depersonalized, mechanistic strategic planning, makes the point that it is people who comprise companies; therefore, in people all value resides. His fellow academic Clive Morton, a business author as well as being a former HR director, says that this observation is "blindingly obvious."

Morton, author of *Becoming World Class* and *Beyond World Class*, which urge manufacturers to integrate people and product development, says there are some positive developments:

"A number of things have helped: the death of strategic planning in terms of being driven by all the numbers and the business of extrapolation from today's figures into the future. All of that has been debunked.

"Henry Mintzberg has helped greatly; he has put forward the philosophy that you cannot predict the future; the nearest you can do is to get a mix of people involved who have a contribution, instead of leaving it to the ivory tower to 'advise' managers. Those ivory tower people have no better perspective than anyone else.

"Mintzberg says that the whole thing is up in the air anyway. Management is not a science; this issue of predicting the future means that you have to analyse trends. Business people have to be, in this sense, much more like politicians, looking at the warp and weft of life; which way the wind is blowing."

Morton argues that "strategy belongs where the action is." He sets out three tenets of this approach:

» the people running a business unit are usually best placed to understand how their markets are developing;
» strategic planning is a continuous evolutionary process; and
» ownership and implementation of strategy are indivisible.[1]

Management theorist Professor Michael Porter has put forward a view that rising living standards depends crucially upon development of specialist skills within particular industries, rather than on macro-economic policies. Those seeking business success and alleviation of poverty should look to human skills, not dry economic theory.

> "To find answers we must focus not on the economy as a whole but on specific industries and industry segments ... The human resources most decisive in modern international competition, for example, possess high levels of specialized skills in particular fields. These are not the result of the general educational system alone but of a process closely connected to competition in particular industries."[2]

He criticizes the classical economic theory that labor behaves like a commodity whose desirability is determined by price. "Nations such as Germany, Switzerland and Sweden have prospered despite high wages and long periods of labour shortage."[3] He also noted that within countries such as the UK, Germany, and Korea, the provinces that were rich in natural resources were actually poorer than other regions. Human resources, typically specializing in a family of skills around business clusters, were the key factor in success.

Dr Pfeffer takes issue similarly with classical theories, which he argues portray a false picture of the world as one of ever-competing interests (see Chapter 8 for a fuller discussion).

Although not formally described as such, there is something of a new school of strategic management in the English-speaking world, independent of the German, Scandinavian, and Japanese experience, which places people development as being integral to general management. The principal thinkers are Pfeffer, Morton, Lynda Gratton of the London Business School, and Mark Huselid, Susan Jackson, and Randall Schuler of Rutgers University. Though each thinker has his or her unique insight, the common principles could be summarized as follows:

» The key to competitive advantage no longer resides in access to capital, in patents or technology or strategic positioning, but in the teamwork and combined skill of the people who comprise the company;

» All strategic decision-making must continually take into account the impact on skills, retention and teamwork, so that people issues are not regarded as being a separate matter;

» A highly committed workforce gives an organization an advantage that is difficult to copy; and

» The influence of classical economic theory on conventional management teaching has taught managers to emphasize that which is measurable, rather than that which is important.

The thinkers argue that conventional management theory and teaching is fundamentally wrong; that it is not enough to move "HR" a little up the agenda. Pfeffer, in his 1994 work *Competitive Advantage Through People*, is withering in his condemnation of accolades granted to the anti-union cost-cutting airline executive Frank Lorenzo, who received an ovation at a talk at Stanford Graduate School of Business in 1989.

"This is the same Frank Lorenzo who, in the decade of the 1980s, took Continental Airlines into bankruptcy twice and led Eastern Airlines to its final demise on 18 January 1991. It is not just any business executive who can take the same company into bankruptcy twice, losing $2.5bn in 1990, and completely ruin what was once the third largest airline in the industry, Eastern."

The explanation of the fêting of Lorenzo lies in the addiction for cost-cutting and classical economics in management thinking, Pfeffer says. Anyone who makes war with the staff is considered a hero, but is damaging the organization. By contrast, Pfeffer notes, Southwest Airlines, with its philosophy of teamwork and staff development, has never had a strike, nor made a loss, since first moving into profit in more than two decades of operations (see case study, Chapter 7).

A study by Mintzberg of failed chief executives found that they had "poor people skills," and that they had "the confidence to make decisions but not the competence to deal with the messy reality in which decisions are executed." The Master of Business Administration, which is "heavy on the business, but light on the administration," is partly to blame.[4]

Recently there has been some implementation of the principles of Pfeffer and Mintzberg. To take the airline industry, British Airways, when appointing Rod Eddington – a former personnel manager – to be chief executive in 2000, made particular reference in the official announcement of his appointment to his people management skills. The carrier had suffered a damaging strike in 1997, which cost an estimated $150 million.

More personnel professionals are beginning to restyle their role as business partners, and are learning more about the roles of the people on the ground; the nature of the services and customers, and the sources of value. They also learn the language of the business and of accountancy, and make a business case. They seek to invert the priority. Instead of seeing themselves as people management experts attached to businesses, they consider themselves business managers with a particular expertise in learning, development, teamwork, and career planning. There is something of a cluster of such managerial approaches in New Zealand, where such HR managers have reached senior executive positions: David Smith, chief executive of the State Insurance Company, George Hickton, chief executive of the New Zealand Tourist Board, and Richard Tweedie, chief executive of Todd Energy; are all former personnel managers who employ this integrationist approach. David Smith comments: "If you have a very motivated staff then that can lead to better customer satisfaction and retention, and profitability."

One of the main thinkers behind such approaches to human resources management is David Ulrich (see Chapter 8).

The modern paradox

Despite all this, progress appears to be patchy. With the weight of research, and a growing body of managers and theorists, arguing that people matters should be integral to management and strategic theory, human resources ought to be center-stage. Yet still it struggles. There is no question that the finance director is on the board, but the HR director? He or she is represented in fewer than half of listed companies.[5] What we have, rather than uniform progress, is new thinking immersed in a postmodern paradox.

Two driving forces of approaches to the management of people have become accentuated in recent years. The forces are the push for higher returns, creating demands for maximum value to be gained from people during the limited time that they work with an organization, versus the force requiring companies to treat people well, as talent and knowledge are the source of all advantage. Such a paradox is accentuated by the fact that the two are not necessarily in fundamental conflict – i.e. getting the maximum value from people during their stay not only necessitates treating them well to a certain degree, but also engaging in the complex task of aligning interests that often overlap, rather than coincide completely. Indeed, management thinkers engage in the study of paradox in their more reflective moments.[6]

Within this dynamic is the struggle of the human resources profession for recognition. Again we encounter a paradox. Many human resources professionals have borrowed the mechanistic analogies and approaches of business process re-engineering with the objective of being more focused on the business, only to find that their solutions from the personnel laboratory are not always suited to the business needs and become dismissed as trendy human resources fads. Examples include 360-degree appraisals or assessment centers – there is nothing wrong with them per se, but they will not be appropriate unless based on a full analysis of people's needs and implemented by line managers who understand and believe in their usefulness, according to many experienced commentators. Martyn Brown, program director of the Advanced Development program at Ashridge Management College in the UK, says that many personnel professionals have an "addiction" to such HR tools. He comments, "A lot of HR people say: 'Look, I've got this tool, I've got to make it fit,' as opposed to saying, 'I don't know what the problem or solution is.'"[7] One of the research studies charting the link between management of people and business success (see Chapter 9, "Links with business performance"), carried out by Watson Wyatt, actually recorded a negative correlation between imposition of certain HR tools and business performance.[8]

Pay systems and training have also come under fire for being too formulaic. Towers Perrin expert Duncan Brown criticizes "Newtonian" assumptions in designing pay and bonus schemes in which "reward lever A is supposed to bring about performance improvement B." He argues that companies should seek motivation and performance improvements through building on the organization's philosophy and sense of purpose, rather than bolting on intricate schemes used elsewhere. Similarly, Alfie Kohn argues in *Punished by Reward* that pay schemes can demotivate by encouraging behavior that people feel bad about. Some extreme forms of performance-related pay for sales teams can even land companies in legal trouble by incentivizing behavior that is dishonest towards customers.[9] (These issues are discussed further in *Motivation Express*. See also *Performance and Reward Management Express*.)

As with reward systems, so it is with training. Criticisms of mechanistic approaches argue that categorization of individual competencies can be limiting, as it introduces a bias towards skills that are more easily observable and measurable, omitting equally important characteristics such as imagination or personality. In such areas as inventions companies, or the caring sector, such intangible entities can be the most important. Paul Kearns, a partner in the independent consultancy Personnel Works, and a staunch critic of such approaches, argues that competencies are particularly inappropriate for managers because "any management population has as many differences as similarities."[10] The biggest drivers are such matters as leadership and initiative, which do not lend themselves readily to the competency approach, he says.

Defenders of competencies, however, say that there is a need to have transferable skills and identify generic learning issues, and that definitions and categorization can help with this. Without this there is a danger that individuals can be equipped only to work in one particular workplace. There is a similarity in the debate on the use of online resources or psychometric tests: that success depends on the wisdom and approach of the people deploying the technique rather than the technique itself (see *Training Express* for further discussion).

Have the Japanese and German partnerships run their course?

Another development possibly holding up application of the integration of personnel and strategic management has been the chequered recent history of Japan and Germany, countries that pioneered such approaches. As discussed in Chapter 3, general management and personnel management are each seen as being part of the other under the approach developed by firms such as Toyota, Nissan, and Honda; while in Germany the policy of *Mitbestimmung* has linked employees and managers together at the major industrial groups.

Problems have been particularly apparent in Japan. The Japanese approach is characterized by emphasis on lifetime employment, job rotation, shared information, collective decision-making, and quality. Lifetime employment has proved particularly difficult to maintain in volatile capital and consumer markets. Some Japanese corporations, having withstood the impulse to make redundancies for most of the 1990s as the nation experienced recessionary conditions, finally began to do so at the end of the decade. In the case of Nissan, the turnaround strategy has been headed by a Westerner, Carlos Ghosn, following the car company's takeover by the French giant Renault in 1999. Research in 1999 and 2000 by Watson Wyatt for the Human Capital Index noted that there was a negative correlation with business performance and job security where that security was not earned through performance (see Chapter 9, "Links with business performance"). Ghosn introduced Western-style individual performance-related pay for managers.

Nissan, among other Japanese firms, was held to be an example of the weakness of the Japanese system, which is that it places too much emphasis on quality of product, while neglecting marketing and strategy. Certainly by the late 1990s it was making an excellent product, but not making profits. Equally, however, it could be argued that marketing and strategy are human skills like any other, and that Nissan was inadequately implementing the Deming philosophy by not including marketers and strategists sufficiently in teamwork. A more serious criticism was that the principle of lifetime employment was held too inflexibly, meaning that poor performers were being tolerated. Other problems with the Japanese and German approaches are discussed in Chapter 3.

No return to "hire and fire"

The travails of some Japanese companies (only some) do not equate to a triumph for those advocating a "hire and fire" approach, however. The vast bulk of value of a company is bound up in its people, especially in the services sector where capital requirements can be low. This has led to businesses engaging in ever-more inventive ways to soften the blow of redundancy or offer alternatives. Certainly the wave of redundancies announced in 2001 was not accompanied by the claims of efficiency gains that accompanied the even more severe exercises in the early 1990s. Managers had suffered serious skills shortages just a few months earlier, and were more reluctant to cut posts. This is not for purely humanitarian concerns: employers know that recessions do not last forever and they will want to have a good reputation when they start hiring again.

One of the most inventive was the example of telecoms group Cisco which, in summer 2001, offered its employees at its San Francisco headquarters the offer of one-third full pay, plus bonuses, if they worked in an approved charity, as an alternative to redundancy. Around 200 members of staff expressed an interest. In 1998 the British luxury car group Rolls-Royce & Bentley made a similar deal with its staff: they could stay at home on full pay during the slack period on the basis that they "banked" their hours to be used in the service of the company later.

If the science of intellectual capital (see below) develops, employers may one day have a reasonably accurate measure of the value of employees that they may be hiring or firing, which probably would create lifetime employment for people who are worth it, while making life even more insecure for those who are not. In the meantime, companies have to guess, and to balance the savings (or apparent savings) from redundancies in the face of collapsing markets with the need to preserve one's reputation as a good employer, and to hold on to valuable skilled people who might be difficult to rehire should the need arise.

Some companies have transformed their recruitment and retention strategies even without firm measures of people's skills. One of the first senior executives to have anticipated this is Bill Gates, who is probably the most assiduous human resources manager in the world. He scours the technology colleges of the world in search of the most gifted people, and has been known to follow up a rejected advance by calling the individual a year or two later to discover if he or she is dissatisfied with the employer they chose instead of Microsoft (see also Chapter 4 and *Recruitment and Retention Express*).

A similar move away from a cost-focused approach to personnel, towards regarding the discipline as adding value, has helped the cause of equal opportunities. By linking greater diversity in employment with greater opportunities for making new customers in ethnic minorities, some companies have moved away from treating the matter as legal compliance. In 2001 the US-based Society for Human Resource Management and the Tanenbaum Center for Inter-religious Understanding carried out research that indicated that employers which accommodate requests on the grounds of religious belief are more likely to keep and motivate staff. In the UK, member-companies of the industry body Race for Opportunity have found that a more diverse workforce has meant more customers. One such firm, the retail bank Lloyds TSB, specifically targeted recruits from the Bangladeshi community in east London, and found that business rose spectacularly as Bangladeshi householders and business people started using the bank's services.[11]

Employee consultation, the unions, and family-friendly policies

In the matter of employee consultation there is still considerable tension. On the one hand, statutory measures guaranteeing workers a say are routinely denounced as a burden upon business by employers' groups; however, on the other hand, the new school of management described earlier in this chapter argue that no elite at the top of the organization can by itself have sufficient knowledge to guide the company. The German Chancellor Gerhard Schröder defended his recent strengthening of works councils by saying that critics overlook their usefulness at times of restructuring, where employee representatives can both offer practical suggestions and carry the workforce along through painful changes.[12] In a less regulated country, the UK, the managers of Rolls-Royce & Bentley acknowledged that the mutually beneficial time-banking deal, referred to above, would not have come about without a partnership arrangement with unions.[13]

So, how important is the distinction between a voluntary approach to participation and one imposed by law? Is consultation good practice, a burden, or a civil entitlement?

Chapter 4 discussed how the spread of technology facilitates communication within an organization. Some research studies indicate that communication is positive. The Human Capital Index, produced by human resources consultancy Watson Wyatt, gives a "score" for employee management, and charts a correlation between these scores and business performance. The research that paved the way for the measure was published in 1999 for North America and in 2000 for Europe. Of the five people management practices that appear to predict an improvement in business performance, one is "communications integrity." As discussed in Chapter 4, the extent of communication or of technology is not as significant as the honesty with which the program is entered into and the priority given to it by senior managers. The Human Capital Index reports thus:

"Communication integrity implies more than information flow. It assumes that communication is candid and open, and reflects a trust and respect among and between managers and employees at all levels of the organization. So significant, in fact, is the integrity of communications that improvement in this area is associated with a 4 per cent increase in a company's market value."[14]

For further discussion on the Human Capital Index, and other research papers showing a link between ways of managing people and business success, go to "Links with business performance," Chapter 9.

The matter of employee communication enters the political arena when business leaders are accused of withholding information from trade unions or employee representative councils before announcing restructurings or redundancies. It is a moot point as to whether this politicization, with the point of view of access to information as being an entitlement, is more or less effective than managerial education encouraging the view that sharing of information is good for the business. Nonetheless, trade union and political protest is inevitable when a company announces closures, especially when the company is large and the region affected is either deprived, overly dependent on the company, or both.

In 1997 the car giant Renault announced the closure of the Belgian car factory in Vilvoorde without fully complying with French or Belgian laws on consultation. A huge political outcry across Europe ensued. The agreement by the European Union in mid 2001 to pass a law requiring all companies with more than 50 employees to consult with the workforce over major restructuring was a direct consequence of the Vilvoorde affair, and would have been approved sooner but for some vigorous opposition from the pan-European employers' group Unice.

Arguments for and against greater consultation are closely mirrored in the debates on the work–life balance. Stronger statutory rights for employees to, for example, parental leave or shorter working hours are opposed by employers' organizations on the grounds of cost, but there is some correlation between family-friendly policies and business success. This is discussed in *Flexible Working*, also in this series.

INTELLECTUAL CAPITAL

In 1992, according to Leif Edvinsson, one of the pioneers of the concept of intellectual capital, the amount of US investment in intangible capital reached the same level ($200 billion) as that in fixed capital. Since then intangibles have outpaced tangibles to the point where, according to accountancy firm Ernst & Young, even a company like BP, with its massive tangible investments, was 75 percent intangible by 1997.[15]

It was a watershed, as significant a turning point for the new economy as the point in the Industrial Revolution in the UK when new conurbations such as Leeds and Manchester became larger than ancient cities such as York and Chester. Yet it is not recognized as such. There is even a backlash against the notion of taking intangible factors into account. The Watson Wyatt Human Capital Index Report – representing one such effort – records the insults heaped upon the discipline:

> "Voodoo economics; bloated balance sheets; Mickey Mouse accounting. Charges like these have often been levelled against efforts to put a value on a company's human capital . . . but few things are more critical than accounting for human capital. It is the chief resource and result of a knowledge-based economy."[16]

Supporters of the importance of intangible capital argue that the fact that something is difficult to measure does not make it cease to exist. If the yawning gap in conventional accounts is not filled by judgment or measurement, then it is filled by guesswork; and to have an approximate gauge of the importance of all key variables is more useful than a precise measure of a select few. As John Maynard Keynes once commented, "It is better to be vaguely right than precisely wrong."

Measuring human capital is difficult because it is not simply the aggregate of the skills of the people in the company at any one point in time (even assuming that these can be quantified). It also depends hugely on the way in which people work together, and the efforts of previous employees in building systems and ways of working that are passed on to new teams. It also includes the value of information that is on databases as well as in people's heads.

Intellectually its history is a little older than some might realize. In 1980 the Japanese theorist Hiroyuki Itami published *Mobilizing Invisible Assets*, although this was not translated into English until 1987. Itami had studied the phenomenon of the collective nature of a successful organization being "more than the sum of its parts" through the intangible benefit of teamworking and established processes. Asset strippers, of course, had long been aware of the reverse situation, but in Japan in the 1970s and 1980s there were few corporations in such straits. Chapter 3 charts the rise of the Japanese manufacturers, and how personnel management was integrated into strategy, and plant management and teamwork, and how knowledge sharing was actively promoted.

In the West several economists, mostly in North America and Sweden, have developed measures for intangible assets. The Swede Karl-Erik Sveiby published *Kunskapsledning* (intellectual capital) in 1990, setting out his accounting principles for the measurement of intangible assets. Leif Edvinsson applied a similar theory when at the insurance group Skandia, producing the first annual report supplement on intellectual capital in 1995 (see Chapter 8 and case study, Chapter 7). His ideas are more than just theory. Around 200 companies, mostly Scandinavian technology companies, pay to have their intellectual capital measured through the consultancy that Edvinsson has set up.[17] One of the most prominent North American thinkers is Baruch Lev, professor at the Stern School of Management at New York University.

Closely related to intellectual capital is the practice of knowledge management – although using Leif Edvinsson's definition this is a constituent part of intellectual capital. Such is the low priority of people management in many firms that some companies have taken the term to mean investing in the best IT networks to help in the sharing of knowledge throughout the organization. As discussed in Chapter 4, however, there is no guarantee that people will volunteer to share information, and the successful applications involve companies providing incentives for people to participate, rather than the slickest technology allowing them to do so.

CONCLUSION

The impact for firms that apply the principles of intellectual capital or the new school of human resources management are profound, because for the first time in accounting and management history people are considered on the positive side of the balance sheet rather than as a cost. And this asset, unlike capital or factories, is mobile, calling for very different, more flexible management skills. As the human resources guru Lynda Gratton, professor of human resources management at the London Business School, pointedly reminds business conferences: "Your employees are volunteers."

There is therefore a fundamental conflict between conventional managerial theory based on classical economics and more humanist approaches aimed at integrating personnel and strategic management. Many, probably most, general managers and many human resources managers employ the former, using mechanistic metaphors that see employees as resources, or commodities. This approach is opposed by the emerging theory put forward by Pfeffer *et al.*, supported by the new discipline of intellectual capital (and practiced by managers such as the trio of New Zealand executives referred to above, and the companies in the case studies in Chapter 7). The force appears to be with the latter group, but redundancy programs, recessionary conditions and problems encountered by the Japanese model are formidable obstacles.

KEY LEARNING POINTS

» People comprise companies and their development can be seen as synonymous with business performance.
» Strategic planning is moving away from ivory towers and precise data; instead, "strategy is where the action is." This ought to put people center-stage.
» Skills are key to regional economic development.
» A new school of management thought is based around the concept of people as the source of competitive advantage.
» This new school is in fundamental opposition to classical economics and traditional management theories, but is applied by some companies.

» Progress for the new approach is patchy. There is an apparent conflict between the new school and the need for cost-control, although this highlights certain paradoxes, rather than a straight-forward conflict of interest.

» Many human resources managers have borrowed the mechanistic analogies of conventional management and have developed "HR tools" that can become fads.

» Pay and training approaches can become too formulaic.

» Problems with the Japanese and German partnership approaches have also been an obstacle. Lifetime employment has drawbacks and may not be practical.

» A few Western companies have sought to minimize the impact of redundancies; they recognize that reputation must stay good and that skilled people represent value.

» Recruitment and retention have been witness to considerable changes away from passive approaches.

» Tensions and paradox emerge in employee consultation: is it good practice, a burden, or a civil right?

» Intellectual capital has emerged as a serious discipline as a means of gauging the value of non-tangible business assets, which now form the majority.

NOTES

1 Morton, C. (1994) *Beyond World Class*. Macmillan Business, London.

2 Porter, M. (1990) *The Competitive Advantage of Nations*. Macmillan, London.

3 Porter, M. (1990) *The Competitive Advantage of Nations*. Macmillan, London.

4 Mintzberg, H. and Lampel, J. (2001) "Do MBAs make better CEOs?" *Fortune*, February 19.

5 See, for example, *Cranet Study 2000*, Cranfield School of Management.

6 Overell, S. (2001) "And now for something completely paradoxical," *Financial Times*, March 14.

7 *Personnel Today*, July 24, 2001, Reed Business Information.

8 Watson Wyatt (2000) *The Human Capital Index Survey Report*. Watson Wyatt.

9 Brown, D. (2001) *Reward Strategies*. CIPD. Pfeffer, J. (1994) *Competitive Advantage Through People*. Harvard Business School Press, Boston.

10 *Personnel Today*, December 5, 2000, Reed Business Information.

11 See www.raceforopportunity.org.uk.

12 "Schröder defends plans to extend codetermination," *Frankfurter Allgemeine*, February 18, 2001.

13 Whiteley, P. (2000) "The end of 'Us and Them'," *The Times*, August 3.

14 Watson Wyatt (2000) *The Human Capital Index Survey Report*. Watson Wyatt.

15 Ernst & Young (1997) *Measures that Matter*. Ernst & Young.

16 Watson Wyatt (2000) *The Human Capital Index Survey Report*. Watson Wyatt.

17 See www.intellectualcapital.se.

People Management in Practice – Success Stories

» Komatsu: unchanging commitment to integrated people and general
  management.
» Southwest Airlines: treating staff as value and serving the customer.
» Skandia: cataloging the range and depth of intellectual capital.

KOMATSU: THE JAPANESE MODEL OF INTEGRATING PEOPLE DEVELOPMENT AND BUSINESS STRATEGY

Industrial manufacturer Komatsu has a long history, having started in the 1920s. It makes primarily bulldozers, tunneling and earth-moving equipment. The company came on to the world stage in the 1960s and 1970s when forced to compete with the US giant Caterpillar as, in 1960, the Japanese government began a staged reduction in import barriers to construction equipment.

In the same year, it began to implement, in common with most Japanese manufacturers, the approach of total quality put forward by the North American thinkers Joseph Juran and W. Edwards Deming. According to business author Clive Morton, former personnel director of Komatsu UK, Japanese firms involved employees and teamwork far more in their approach to total quality than most Western firms that introduced the idea in the 1980s.[1]

Progress in the early 1960s was rapid, as commented years later by the management gurus Gary Hamel and C.K. Prahalad: "When Komatsu set its goal to match Caterpillar's world-class quality in 1960, its product quality was less than half that of its exemplar. A more realistic goal . . . might have been a 20 percent annual improvement in quality, but this would have left it far short of what it needed to wrest share from Caterpillar in export markets. Komatsu did achieve world-class quality levels . . . a mere three years after announcing its quality quest."[2]

In 1984 the company stepped up its overseas operations. The 1985 Plaza Accord approved the appreciation of the yen, which made exporting more expensive for Japanese firms. Komatsu had anticipated such a move, and established Komatsu America Manufacturing and Komatsu UK in 1984 as overseas manufacturing bases. This was followed by rapid expansion in Europe, the Americas, and southeast Asia.

In 1989 Tetsuya Katada became president. His stewardship saw an intensification of the focus on improvements in product both through, and alongside, improvements in internal communication and employee development. This was accompanied by a move towards globalization, with the establishment of manufacturing plants throughout the world.

Katada, in keeping with the Japanese manufacturers' policy of rotating managers in preparation for senior roles, had spent a time as a personnel manager. His career gives an illustration of a half-century's worth of combining personnel and general management in the Japanese system, and is typical of many senior Japanese industrialists. He joined Komatsu in 1954, starting in the human resources division at the Osaka plant. He served in different management roles, principally personnel, before becoming a director in 1978. In 1983 he was appointed a managing director at the group, rising to vice-president in 1988 and president (representative director) a year later.

Katada's philosophy is based on the principles of fairness and motivation, and placing these as being central to the business, not as "add-ons" invented by a segregated human resources department. "Motivation is the key to get the best and most potential out of people," he comments. "You should know, however, that the ways to motivate people are different for each person."

Simultaneously, from his appointment in 1989, he set about developing a more strategic outlook for the company as a whole, which meant everyone knowing about, and being encouraged to contribute to, the company's direction. He argued that management had become obsessed with Caterpillar and had stopped thinking about strategic choice; they had neglected the lower end of the market. He decided that you can no longer operate within the confines defined by the objectives – managers need to be innovative, always encouraging initiative from below.

Clive Morton commented:

"He stressed the link between business development and product development with listening to the customer, and also getting ideas from within the company. He wanted everyone to stop concentrating on catching up with Caterpillar. As HR director it was very clear that I had full responsibilities for business success, like any other director, and that the concerns over people management were shared by my Japanese colleagues. There is an enormous difference to the situation where you're the HR director and are expected to solve other people's problems and pour oil on troubled waters."

Single status and communication

As with other Japanese manufacturers, Komatsu operates a single-status policy, doing away with white collar/blue collar class distinctions. This facilitates communication, as the employees on the shop floor can see and come to know senior managers as they wear the same clothes and eat in the same canteen. But the thinking goes deeper. Single status helps multi-skilling and flexibility, as it can create incentives to train: an operative skilled in a certain discipline can be confident that he or she will be treated in the same way and under the same pay and bonus system if transferring to another section or adding a new skill. There is encouragement for movement throughout the company, in contrast with a common assumption in many companies that the only route for self-betterment lies in management. For example, it is common in Komatsu for people to move from lower-skilled jobs such as painting and welding into more highly technical positions in design. Others can gain skills and extra income by developing training skills while staying within their team and primary role. Such policies, by maximizing internal recruitment, can save on costs as well as reducing the potential for skills shortages.

During its rapid expansion across the globe in the 1980s and 1990s the company had a policy of deliberately keeping staff numbers quite lean in the early stages of setting up a new plant. This was not simply to reduce costs, but to try to maximize the productivity and participation of the people who were hired, and to minimize the need to make redundancies should the subsidiary be hit by difficult trading conditions. The philosophy is that "if the company grows, you grow, and the company will grow because you grow."[3] Single status has now been extended to many service sector companies in the West (*The Times*, July 26, 2001).

There is also intensive training in people management skills for supervisors of teams. Individuals go to the Japanese headquarters for training in recruitment, appraisal, and people development skills. The emphasis is on "listening and learning," which involves, in some cases, a conscious move away from "correcting and directing" as a mode of leadership. Communication is emphasized generally through a five- to ten-minute briefing for all staff at the changeover of a shift. In addition – in common with many modern manufacturers – the company has quality circles. Komatsu seeks to ensure that these inter-disciplinary groups of people are responsible for generating ideas for improvements to processes and products, as well as monitoring the quality of the existing output.

Clive Morton commented:

> "One thing that has struck me about the Japanese firms is that if you talk to them, however far down the organization's hierarchy, they would all know the commercial situation of the company; they would all be sensitive to the pinch points; the market penetration of such and such a machine. When there was a new product coming out they would know the customer view about the old one."

Timeline

» **1960**: Japanese government permits Caterpillar to import to Japan. Komatsu begins total quality management.
» **1976**: Opens plant in Mexico.
» **1984**: US and British manufacturing subsidiaries opened.
» **1985**: Appreciation of yen agreed.
» **1989**: Tetsuya Katada appointed president. Begins focus on innovation and involvement of staff in strategy.
» **1990s**: Globalization continues and strengthens through the decade.

KOMATSU: KEY INSIGHTS

» The most senior executive officer has experience of personnel, and insight into matters such as teamwork and motivation.
» Internal communication has been emphasized as an integral part of moves towards globalization.
» Single status encourages flexible working and multi-skilling.
» There is a strong emphasis on teamwork.
» All line managers have intensive training in management of people.
» There is an explicit and continual emphasis on "listening and learning," as opposed to "correcting and directing."

> » Staff at all levels in the organization have knowledge of the customer and of the market.

SOUTHWEST AIRLINES: THE US MODEL OF SERVING THE CUSTOMERS BY SERVING THE EMPLOYEES

On June 18, 1971 Herb Kelleher, an attorney, and businessman Rollin King created the first budget airline, Southwest Airlines, connecting Dallas, Houston, and San Antonio in the southern USA. From its inception it has placed employee welfare and development as being at the heart of its approach. Its philosophy comes not from a management guru, nor a motivational psychologist, nor an esoteric organizational theory, but from Jesus Christ. The modus operandi is: "Treat people as you would like to be treated." This extends internally to all employees, and externally to all customers.

Within three years of its first flight, the airline carried its millionth customer, and was operating profitably. Today, nearly 64 million passengers use the airline annually – making it the fourth largest in the United States. In 2001, Southwest Airlines was celebrating 28 consecutive years of profitability.

The Website tells us:

"At Southwest Airlines, the Customer always comes first. So do our Employees. To underscore this philosophy, we always capitalize the 'C' in 'Customer' and the 'E' in 'Employee.' Paychecks are signed 'From Our Customers,' and all Employees from ground operations to flight attendants are well versed in delivering Positively Outrageous Service."

The company declines to refer to its staff as resources, assets or commodities, arguing that this is dehumanizing. Hence it renamed its personnel department to people department in 1989. At the same time, it introduced a corporate university to carry out the intensive training courses that staff go through. Donna Conover, vice-president of customer service and people, comments:

"We have always thought that if we please the customer first, before they demand it, then we save everyone a lot of inconvenience or aggravation, and we instill this in our employees. It starts with your leadership group doing it for the employee group: when an employee wants something and goes to a supervisor or manager or director or vice-president that person is available and helps solve the issue and concern."

These principles are ingrained in those trained for leadership positions; the values are instilled at every stage of development, training and promotion. This is partly self-sustaining, because new employees can see that those who seek to treat people well and be a servant to their needs are those who gain promotion. This is integral to the business education, not separate. "You have to teach people in the business world how to make good decisions, along with treating people well," says Conover.

Training has a high priority with the airline and on the courses, too, it is hoped that people will have fun as well as learn. In 1995 standard training was increased from three weeks to four-and-a-half weeks. This was partly to include extra factual instruction on new services – for example the medical service that enabled staff to contact a doctor from an aircraft – and partly also to reflect increased regulations affecting the airline industry. But another reason for the expansion was to include more on customer service.

The four-and-a-half weeks' basic training covers intensive courses on customer service, the aircraft, safety, and regulations. The training includes three days on teaching on the culture of working at the company and on customer service. There is one such course every month, with around 200 people attending. The drop-out rate is 15 percent, but almost all the remaining trainees are accepted as employees on a probationary basis.

The trickle-down personality

Besides being smart, efficient, and dedicated, Southwest Airlines' employees are expected to have fun. Humor is an essential element throughout Southwest's system, from Herb Kelleher, the maverick chief executive who has been known to dress up like Elvis, belt out a rap song, and settle a dispute by arm-wrestling, down to all levels. Employees have been known to tell silly jokes, and even sing in-flight instructions to customers.

Recruitment is a massively important exercise for Southwest Airlines. Each employee is carefully hand-picked from more than 100,000 applications submitted each year. In 1999, for example, it interviewed 80,000 people in order to fill 4,200 openings. The huge number of applicants is maintained despite the fact that those successful at an initial interview then undergo four-and-a-half weeks' training without pay. This high level of applicants was maintained even as unemployment dipped to historic lows in the USA in 1999 and 2000.

Those who complete their training are then on probation for six months. Initial recruitment is based largely on personality, as the company looks for people who will work hard, but also have a natural desire to please people, to communicate, and to have a positive outlook. It regards this filtering as a very important feature of the business. If someone shows positive attributes, but indicates an unwillingness to work with the firm after six months, Southwest Airlines will help the individual find a new job.

Punctually each month the company's "Employee of the Month" is named and details of the individual's contribution posted on the Website. This includes a color photograph and extended written profile.

In May 1988, Southwest Airlines became the first airline to win the US industry's "Triple Crown" in one month – best on-time record, best baggage handling, and fewest customer complaints. Since then it has won it more than thirty times, as well as five annual Triple Crowns for 1992, 1993, 1994, 1995, and 1996. Its annual staff turnover is 9 percent, which is considerably lower than the industry average. It is sixth on the *Fortune* list of most admired companies.

The company inverts the onus that is common with many employers. Instead of using customer needs and demands as a stick with which to beat the staff, it seeks to enthuse staff to want to please the customers. This is more rewarding from the flight staff's point of view, and more sustainable from the managers' point of view.

The company has never had a strike, even though it is highly unionized and labor disputes have been a common feature of airlines in North America. Senior managers are neutral on union membership; neither promoting it nor dissuading employees. It places a high priority on communication with employees. "What we remember, when dealing with unions, is that they are our employees first," says Donna Conover. "If you treat them that way then you can disagree but if we honor the contract you really do not have as many issues."

Communication with the staff is important. There is a weekly newsletter for each department; there are monthly updates from the communications department for all employees, and the Website is continually updated. If there is to be a major announcement, care is taken to ensure that the employees are the first to know. This deals with a frequent cause of disenchantment and sometimes industrial action at other employers (see "Employee consultation, the unions, and family-friendly policies," Chapter 6), particularly if staff have read about a change in the newspaper before hearing anything directly from senior managers.

Southwest Airlines does not see the expense of recruiting and paying staff as being net cost, which is still the implicit assumption of some organizations. Instead it is seen as a core investment. For example, in a revealing comment from the airline's finance vice-president Gary Kelly, he noted that some investors from time to time put pressure on him to reduce the amount the company spends annually on recruitment and selection of staff. He says: "I do get asked on occasion by investors, 'Could you cut your costs in this area?' But if you are not going to work hard to get people who are a good fit, it will hurt you. For example, we have never had a strike. What airline is even close to being able to say that?"[4]

The example of Southwest Airlines proves that it is possible to be strategic in people management and in the general approach to business, while remaining informal and accessible. Despite its informal appearance, it is a highly disciplined organization. What distinguishes it from many employers is that it treats recruitment and training of staff with great seriousness and consistency, and places these matters at the heart of business, rather than the periphery.

Timeline

» **1971**: Herb Kelleher and Rollin King set up Southwest Airlines, serving three cities.

» **1975**: Company introduces hostess of the month, later employee of the month.
» **1988**: Southwest wins the "triple crown" for airline service for the first time.
» **1989**: The start of the company's university.
» **1989**: The personnel department is renamed the people department.
» **1995**: Standard training increased from three weeks to four-and-a-half weeks, partly to increase training in customer service and the company culture.
» **2000**: Reaches number six spot in the *Fortune* list of most admired companies.

SOUTHWEST AIRLINES: KEY INSIGHTS

» Integration of people development and customer service is based on a Biblical principle; there are no complex matrices or organizational models.
» There is an explicit rejection of the concept of staff as resources or commodities.
» Considerable investment is ploughed into recruitment and training.
» A strong reputation as a desirable place to work can keep applicants flowing in during a time of full employment.
» Senior managers are trained to serve more junior employees and meet their needs.
» Employees are the first to be told when a major change is being prepared.

Note: a longer case study on Southwest Airlines can be read in Harris, J. (1996) *Getting Employees to Fall in Love With Your Company*, Amacon, New York.

SKANDIA: THE SCANDINAVIAN APPROACH TO VALUING PEOPLE THROUGH A MEASURE OF INTELLECTUAL CAPITAL

Swedish insurance group Skandia established its intellectual capital in 1991, appointing Leif Edvinsson as vice-president with responsibility in this area (see "Key thinkers," Chapter 8). From the start, Edvinsson describes the approach as a fundamental rethinking of the organization, looking at employees, their ways of working, and their shared knowledge as the fundamental asset of the company, which is not recorded on conventional accounts. He set about re-orientating the company to one focused on assets and on the future, rather than on costs and on the past.

His close intellectual colleague Karl-Erik Sveiby describes it thus: "Money is merely a proxy for human effort, and the 500-year-old system of accounting sheds little light on the vital processes in organizations whose assets are largely non-monetary."[5]

Sveiby goes further, criticizing the unfavorable accounting treatment of investing in people, compared with investing in technology. Investment in a new IT system is recorded as a negative cash flow, but the acquisition is chalked up as an asset on the balance sheet. By contrast investment in training appears as both cash loss and as expenditure – even though it can be as useful, or more so, to profit-making capability.

Working on these principles in the early 1990s, Edvinsson was able, by 1994, to produce the world's first intellectual capital report, which was publicly available. This followed years of developing the measuring and the IT systems necessary, and also winning over hearts and minds to a very different way of viewing the organization and of managing. Prototype intellectual capital reports were produced every six months or so.

Edvinsson divides market capital into financial capital and intellectual capital. The latter is then sub-divided into human capital and structural capital. This is the distinction between the capabilities of teams within the organization, and matters such as knowledge on the database or ways of working that have been developed and embedded into the organization. Assessors use the tools developed by Edvinsson to give ratings for the different departments, teams, and even individuals in the organization according to how well they score against benchmarks.

As such, Skandia's intellectual capital department was a combination of human resources, IT, and finance, but within this new orientation, which meant a fundamental reshaping of the priorities of the three core disciplines. There was a fair amount of inertia in the organization,

Edvinsson reports, making it difficult to change ways of working in traditional departments, even when the intellectual arguments had been largely won, simply because it was such a profound change. For example, financial controllers had to be convinced that employing several people simply to measure and keep up to date the intellectual capital ratings was a worthwhile investment. Skandia currently employs around 100 people to do this.

But the measurement simply gives people a language, Edvinsson says; the more important change is a conceptual change in seeing people and groups of people as assets capable of continual development.

Effects on business and management of people were dramatic, however. Recruitment was made easier because Skandia immediately gained a reputation as an innovative company. Edvinsson comments:

> "Traditional leadership is very much focused on getting people to work more. And there is very much a limit to how much people can work; if it is beyond a limit of ten hours a day it is very close to burn-out. Therefore you have to replace the work component with structural capital."

Using this concept, and the measures, Skandia is better able to identify its embedded strengths and weaknesses. This can help identify where it has the in-house expertise and where it might be advantageous to buy in a system or strike a partnership with another company. By contrast, using traditional accountancy-based managerial models it is assumed that people are a cost, and so there is a tendency to look at processes, at increasing working hours or reducing headcount in a two-dimensional analysis, rather than examining the strengths of the teams and having a measure for the benefits as well as the costs that they represent.

At Skandia, one of the main innovations in terms of people management was the development of "competency insurance" for individuals, modelled on health or life insurance and reflecting the reality that one's livelihood in the knowledge economy derives from one's ability and the capacity to develop and learn. This works like an individual training levy – the employee pays in 5 percent of salary, matched by the employer, to pay for training; which could amount to as much as a year's sabbatical to take a Master's degree. "Most people's capacity is eroding from a knowledge point of view, leading to an increase in burn-out," says Edvinsson.

By 1998 Skandia had fully installed its Dolphin communication system. This facilitated internal communication between teams, and also gave them information on their development. So an individual on behalf of him or herself, or on behalf of their team, can look up their intellectual capital rating as it develops through time. It also makes available ratings on customer relationships and innovative capacity.

Business improved markedly throughout the 1990s. The calibration of customer capital within the ratings for intellectual capital helped change the focus of the company strategy from the financial markets towards the customer. It encouraged senior managers to focus on the fact that Skandia had one or two traditional products and only 0.1 percent of the Swedish market. This led to the development of new products, reducing the company's reliance on investments that were prone to sudden changes in worldwide interest rates. By 1996 it had leapt from 300th place in the rankings of insurance companies in the country – its position in the early 1990s – to third place.

To help its innovative capacity, Skandia set up a Future Center, where people discuss potential trends in society and in the economy so as to try to anticipate them as an employer and a provider of services. People will discuss developments in the insurance market, but also new technology and different ways of working together.

Edvinsson comments:

"The innovation dimension, from an accounting viewpoint, is investment at the end [of the business cycle]. First you harvest and if there is enough there might be some investment going in; but this is a dangerous approach, because it might be that you consume too much and invest too little. The logic required is to visualize how much you are devoting to innovation; making systems around innovation, and looking at time to market and speed of renewal."

Timeline

» **1991**: Skandia sets up function of intellectual capital. Leif Edvinsson appointed director.

» **1991–4**: Criteria and measurements established; IT systems developed to support them.
» **1994**: First public statement of intellectual capital.
» **1996**: Skandia becomes third in market share in Sweden.
» **1996**: The company begins its "competency insurance" service for staff, later marketed externally.
» **1998**: "Dolphin" knowledge sharing system completed.

SKANDIA: KEY INSIGHTS

» There has been a deliberate and strategic effort to measure the contribution of people.
» Measurement of intellectual capital has been integrated into different managerial emphases, rather than stand as an exercise in itself.
» There is a systematic approach to looking at the strengths of groups and teams.
» Links are made to customers and to innovation, which has led to new products and a much stronger market share.
» The mere fact of being seen to be innovative in using intellectual capital has helped recruitment.
» Internal communication and optimum use of technology are emphasized, which gives managers and other staff a continually updated picture of their development and developmental needs.
» The new approach to management takes in the dimension of time – of past development and future potential – which is missing from the conventional balance sheet. This has helped organic growth.

NOTES

1 Morton, C. (1994) *Becoming World Class*. Macmillan Business, London.
2 Hamel, G. and Prahalad, C.K. (1994) *Competing for the Future*. Harvard Business Press, Boston.
3 Morton, C. (1994) *Becoming World Class*. Macmillan Business, London.

4 See *CFO* (magazine for senior financial officers), March 2000.
5 Sveiby, K-E. (1998) *Measuring Intangibles and Intellectual Capital – An Emerging First Standard*, www.sveiby.com.au/EmergingStandard.html; see also Sveiby, K-E. (1997) *The New Organizational Wealth – Managing and Measuring Knowledge-Based Assets*. Berret-Koehler, San Francisco.

Key Concepts and Thinkers in People Management

» A–Z listing of key terms and concepts in the management of people.
» Key thinkers: Jeffrey Pfeffer; Leif Edvinsson; Randall Schuler and Susan Jackson; and Dave Ulrich.

GLOSSARY

Adding value – This is the newest and most significant phrase to have entered discussion on the role of the personnel department. It has followed from the teaching of Dave Ulrich (see "Key thinkers" below) who argues that, to survive, human resources departments have to be of demonstrable benefit to the functioning of the business as a whole. The idea is that HR professionals should start with the business objective, say, customer service staff with better product knowledge to improve customer retention, and work back to the training and development program required. Too often they have begun with the solution – an off-the-shelf training or appraisal program – and imposed it on the business.

Balanced scorecard – This is similar to intellectual capital and represents an attempt to encourage managers to measure the business against a range of yardsticks, rather than just financial returns. It was developed by Robert Kaplan and David Norton. Typically, the scorecard includes customer satisfaction, employee satisfaction, quality of service, response times, and so on. The idea is not to diminish the importance of profitability and return to shareholders, but to recognize that strong financial performance is often the by-product of getting the other aspects right. See www.balancedscorecard.com.

Compensation and benefits – See Performance and reward management.

Diversity – Increasingly for international firms the pool of available talent is global, as trade barriers come down, education standards improve in many countries, and multinationals want to recruit people with knowledge of local markets. It has also become evident that, in addition to the questions of fairness and equal rights, an ethnically diverse, gender-balanced workforce can be more versatile, as it incorporates a wider range of cultural viewpoints and hence potential solutions to problems. See also Chapter 5 and *Diversity Express*.

Emotional Intelligence – The move away from "command and control" structures in many organizations implies different managerial skill requirements. Emotional intelligence refers to the ability to communicate, empathize, and enthuse, as opposed to the traditional disciplines of analysis and decision-making.[1] It is also thought that women are more likely to display emotional intelligence than men, making a case for a more diverse managerial population.

Flexible Working – Use of the term "flexibility" demands great care in the context of employment, as it has flexible definitions itself. In political discussions the term "flexible labor markets" has often been interpreted as meaning those with weak trade unions, whose flexibility is to suit the needs of employers. However, flexible working can be used to mean the opposite: flexible hours to suit the needs of staff, especially those with families. Some employers see a synthesis of these twin demands: that they offer opportunities for some choice over hours and conditions in return for commitment to respond to urgent demands where it is in the company's interests. Many find that such a trade-off is more likely to yield true responsiveness than demanding that staff always be there at the management's behest. The term *flexible benefits* refers to allowing employees some say over their perks allowing them to trade in pension contributions for extra holiday, for example. See *Flexible Working Express*, and *Performance and Reward Express*, also in this series.

Intellectual capital – This is a more arithmetical approach to the ideas expressed in the balanced scorecard. It is an attempt to give managers a measure of the strength of embedded knowledge, teamwork and collective ability of an organization. This is more likely to be an indicator of the ability of an organization to achieve its goals than financial results, which are historical and only measure transactions and fixed assets. A company can now have its intellectual capital measured by the Swedish company intellectualcapital.se. It takes around six weeks and entails assessors asking questions and grading employers on their human resources practices, technological infrastructure, and organizational systems. See Leif Edvinsson under "Key thinkers" (below), and Chapter 6, "Intellectual capital".

Motivation – Psychological literature on motivation of individuals and groups at work now extends over nearly a century, and has influenced management education and workplace organization. The seminal work was the Hawthorne Experiment in the 1920s by Elton Mayo. This strongly indicated that physical environment had negligible effect on productivity and that group dynamics hold the key. See *Motivation Express*, also in this series, and Chapter 3.

Performance and reward management – Pay has varied in its place in the hierarchy of matters to concern those responsible for management of people. The fathers of scientific management, Henry Ford and Frederick Taylor, in the early part of the twentieth century, argued that pay was the main motivating factor. Ford once commented that "Men work for two reasons: pay and the fear of losing one's job." Since then many psychological theories have focused on values and the intrinsic purpose of a job, implying that pay is less important. In the 1950s Frederick Herzberg introduced the concept of "hygiene" factors, including pay and working conditions, which have the potential to cause dissatisfaction if not right but which were distinct from motivating factors. Recently, however, it is felt that pay cannot be neatly separated from motivation, nor from the new discipline of performance management, which concerns the integration of appraisal, performance monitoring, career development, and remuneration. See *Performance and Reward Management Express*, and *Motivation Express*, also in this series.

Recruitment and retention – After decades as a junior discipline, recruitment and retention shot to the top of the agenda in the late 1990s, when skills shortages affected most employers, particularly in the high-technology areas. The "war for talent" became real, as telecoms companies openly poached individuals from competitors and used technology to trace software developers who had set up their own Websites, or track individuals who had browsed their situations vacant page. Even though many firms have made redundancies since, many have put great emphasis on retaining the most important skills. See Chapter 6 and *Recruitment and Retention Express*.

Strategic partner – This is closely related to the concept of added value (see above), and concerns the role that many senior personnel professionals seek to have with the board. In the past the human resources department has often followed its own agenda, rather than be tied in to the business objectives. Increasingly it is held that people management improvements can only occur if they tally with the culture and objectives of the business. See Dave Ulrich (below) and Chapter 6, "People move center stage".

Teamworking – Many business re-engineering programs since the early 1990s have taken out layers of management hierarchy from organizations, while newer start-ups have deliberately maintained single status for employees, first-name terms, and a flat hierarchy. New technology also tends to reduce low-skilled jobs and facilitates communication between professionals of a similar discipline in different locations. Joint ventures have become common. All of these trends mean that teamworking abilities are essential in most organizations; they also mean that ability to manage people is more important for line managers. There are numerous psychometric tests to gauge people's propensity for working in teams; the most well-known are Belbin and Myers-Briggs, which give an indication, among other matters, as to one's disposition to work singly or in teams. The concept of emotional intelligence (see above) is aimed at helping managers coach and nurture teams, rather than just issue instructions. See *Teamworking Express*, also in this series.

Training and development – The oldest discipline in the management of people has suffered from a lowly image in managerial circles, though with the exception of France and Germany, where it has always had a high priority, reflected in strong state education systems and training levies for employers. The advent of the "knowledge economy" has given its profile a boost, and it has been assisted also by the increased access to training and development through the Internet and intranets. See Chapter 4 and *Training and Development Express*.

KEY THINKERS

Edvinsson, Leif

Leif Edvinsson, chief executive of Universal Networking Intellectual Capital and board member of several knowledge-based companies, is one of the pioneers of intellectual capital, the practice of giving organizations a measure of their intangible assets. He was not the first thinker, but he was the first to apply the young theory in the workplace during his spell in the 1990s with Sweden-based life assurance firm Skandia (see Chapter 7).

He was appointed to Skandia in 1991 as vice-president of intellectual capital, the first such post in the corporate world. Four years later he produced the first public statement on intellectual capital on behalf of the company. His patented measure is now used by around 200 employers, mostly IT firms in Scandinavia.[2] In 2001 he was appointed to the world's first professorship in intellectual capital at the University of Lund.

Before joining Skandia in 1991, he was senior vice-president for training and development at S-E Bank, after being president and chairman of Consultus, a Stockholm-based consulting company.

Edvinsson argues that managers using conventional accounting to make decisions are only looking at historic transactions and fixed assets – in other words, between 1 percent and 25 percent of the value of the company. This can lead them to make serious, even disastrous errors, particularly on downsizing and merging, where they are failing to take the intangible value of teamwork and skills into account.

Despite its term, the concept of intellectual capital is not only legitimate for high-tech and research consultancies. "Intellectual capital is an approach for all companies," he says. "Most companies have intangible assets and the other aspect is that it [this approach] is about future earnings potential. It is a 180-degree perception shift from traditional accounting and historical cost accounting which is looking backwards."

He divides intellectual capital into three dimensions: efficiency, renewal, and risk. This attempts to codify, in a balanced way, the complex interplay of the components of an organization's intangible assets – the skills and teamwork of the current workforce; the knowledge on databases; the systems and ways of working that are inherited, and the possibility that any of these may be lost.

See Edvinsson, L. and Malone, M. (1997) *Intellectual Capital*, Harper-Collins, New York, and www.intellectualcapital.se.

Pfeffer, Jeffrey

Jeffrey Pfeffer is a professor of organizational behavior at Stanford University in the US. He has carried out numerous research studies charting the correlation between human resources policies and business success. He is a critic of mechanistic analogies and argues that the commitment and teamwork of the workforce are the decisive competitive factors, not processes or systems.

For an academic, Dr Pfeffer is blunt in his critique of "hire and fire" approaches to management, which he argues are fundamentally wrong. His philosophy is that staff are not a resource, but are instead the sole means of profit-making, because they comprise the organization. Companies that place their well-being and development as being integral to the underlying principles and strategic decision-making consistently outperform others.

His influential 1994 work *Competitive Advantage Through People* includes the chapter "Wrong heroes, wrong theories, wrong language" in which he states that "The business press and business executives, who make heroes out of people who exemplify the opposite of the qualities and behavior necessary to achieve success through people, make it harder for a different way of management to emerge." Pfeffer records the way in which many business journals and Wall Street investors lionize cost-cutting executives with an appalling record of business failure. In *Competitive Advantage* he singles out the record of Frank Lorenzo at different North American airlines, who received a standing ovation from business students despite leading one company into bankruptcy and another perilously close in the 1980s (see Chapter 6).

He criticizes agency theories and transaction cost economics, both based on classical economics, for resulting in a mechanistic way of viewing organizational behavior. This leads to inaccurate models of people as self-interested economic units uninterested in co-operating. It also leads to desperate attempts to solve resulting human relations problems through pay systems that are based on punishment and reward. The assumption of mutually opposing interests, accompanied by military metaphors and "war-like language," results in a deliberately confrontational approach to employee relations, he argues. This can lead to self-fulfilling prophecies – in other words, tell the workforce and the union that they are the shareholders' enemy often enough and they will behave as though they are.

He also challenges the classical economics notion that labor behaves like a commodity and that therefore competitive advantage ought to accrue from reducing its cost. Not only is this not the case – many high-wage economies are very competitive – but reducing rates does not even reduce direct labor costs in many cases, because of the hidden costs of strikes and higher staff turnover.

Dr Pfeffer gained his PhD in Business Administration from the Stanford Graduate School of Business. He is a member and fellow of the Academy of Management and a member of the Industrial Relations Research Association. He has taught executive seminars in 26 countries and serves on the boards of several companies (a full CV is at http://faculty-gsb.stanford.edu/pfeffer/).

Dr Pfeffer has authored or co-authored ten books, some of which are on the subject of organizational theory. Those that most concern personnel management are:

» *Managing with Power: Politics and Influence in Organizations* (1992). Harvard Business School Press, Boston.
» *Competitive Advantage Through People* (1994). Harvard Business School Press, Boston.
» *The Human Equation: Building Profits by Putting People First* (1998). Harvard Business School Press, Boston.
» *The Knowing-Doing Gap: How Smart Companies Turn Knowledge into Action* (1999). Harvard Business School Press, Boston.
» *Hidden Value: How Great Companies Achieve Extraordinary Results with Ordinary People* (2000). Harvard Business School Press, Boston.

Schuler, Randall and Jackson, Susan

These two professors from Rutgers University, New Jersey, USA, specialize in identifying the particular approaches to personnel management that are needed to ensure an effective link with the rest of the business. Their advice is tailored towards senior executives who wish to embed development of people more closely with the setting of strategy. Only by doing this can organizations be truly responsive and innovative, they argue.

The factor that distinguishes learning companies from other companies is the capacity to "combine an ability to manage knowledge with an ability to change continuously so as to improve their effectiveness. Knowledge is needed for learning, but is not sufficient." They employ the acronym LEARN to help executives turn organizations into learning organizations. It stands for: Leverage – the orientation of learning capabilities towards meeting the needs of stakeholders; Embed – the inculcation of a culture that is difficult to imitate; Accessible – referring to the importance of access to training for all; Renew – the discipline of continual monitoring of information from customers and other constituencies; and Non-financial measurement – which refers to such measures as the balanced scorecard or intellectual capital.[3]

They are positive about the prospects for companies adopting such approaches. They argue that the integration of people management and strategic management is happening inexorably as companies identify their unique, inimitable source of competitive strength to come from skills, knowledge systems, and teamwork, rather than from patents, access to capital, strategic positioning, or the big idea: "Increasingly the HR department is being recognized as an asset to the strategic planning process, since it is both the locus of implementation of the strategic plans ... and a valuable source of knowledge about the internal and external environment."[4]

Professor Schuler argues that the lessons of excessive downsizing and failed mergers have forced the issue of people development and organizational culture on to the agenda for top management: "So many of the failures seem to be related to people or the cultures of the two different companies. The whole evolution of mergers and acquisitions and international joint ventures has given more publicity to the importance of people in the success of the organization."

Schuler adds that high-profile successful executives, such as Bill Gates and Jack Welch, have committed time and resources to education, recruitment and training, particularly of technical people and management. The benefits of Jack Welch's management training center for General Electric at Crotonville have become popularized through the media; and employers want to appear in lists such as the "top 100 companies to work for" that are read by graduates. One *Business Week* feature reckoned that Welch spends up to half his time on "people" issues.[5]

The importance of linking personnel with strategy is also emphasized by such management gurus as Gary Hamel and Michael Porter, says Professor Schuler, and is being taken seriously by the personnel management professional associations that each country has.

Schuler and Jackson have published numerous books and academic articles including the following:

» Schuler, R.S. and Jackson, S.E. (1987) "Linking competitive strategies with human resource management practices," Academy of Management Executive, pp. 207-219.

» Schuler, R.S. (1992) "Strategic human resources management: linking the people with the strategic needs of the business," *Organizational Dynamics*, pp. 18-32.

» Schuler, R.S. and Jackson, S.E. (1997) "Linking competitive strategies with human resource management practices," *Academy of Management Executive*, August, pp. 207-219.

» Schuler, R.S. and Jackson, S.E. (1999) *Strategic Human Resource Management: A Reader*. Blackwell, London.

» Schuler, R.S. and Jackson, S.E. (2001) "Turning knowledge into business advantage," *Financial Times*, January 15.

» Schuler, R.S. and Jackson, S.E. (2001) "Human resource management: past, present and future," in *Comparative Labor Law and Industrial Relations* (7th edn), Kluwer Law International, The Hague.

Ulrich, David

Ulrich is professor at Michigan Business School, and was listed by *Business Week* magazine as one of the world's top ten executive educators in 1993. He is a popular conference speaker, bringing a charismatic style of delivery and generating audience participation.

His analysis is similar to that of Schuler and Jackson (see above) but his focus is slightly different in that he analyzes the particular skills and development needs of the human resources professionals, rather than those of the senior executive or the board. He has defined four main roles for the personnel profession, which are: the strategic partner, the employee champion, the administrator, and the change agent. Ideally an organization should have all four, and with equal status, he argues, and all with the basic orientation of helping the organization as a whole meet the needs of the customers, investors, and employees.

Ulrich accepts the common criticisms of human resources departments – that they are too bound up in perfecting their own procedures and insufficiently focused on the business needs (see Chapter 6, "The modern paradox"). Indeed, he even dares to ask: "Should we do away with HR?"[6] But Ulrich argues that the need for good people management approaches has never been stronger, and that both senior executives and the personnel professionals have to change, so that the function is, and is seen to be, adding value to the business. Competitive success is a function of overall organizational excellence, he argues, so senior executives and line managers should use the human resources department, hold it to account, and understand the importance of the development of staff – just as much as the HR professionals need to learn the business objectives.

The HR Scorecard, co-authored with Mark Huselid and Brian Becker, concerns the importance of people management to business success and offers a method to gauge the effects of the contribution of the human resources policies on the effectiveness of the organization. As such, it is similar to approaches to intellectual capital (see Leif Edvinsson, above, and Chapter 6, "Intellectual capital"). Books and articles by Ulrich include the following:

» Ulrich, D. and Lake, D. (1990) *Organizational Capability: Competing from the Inside Out.* Wiley, New York.
» Ulrich, D., Ashkenas, R., Kerr, S. and Jick, T. (1995) *The Boundaryless Organization Breaking the Chains of Organization Structure.* Jossey-Bass, San Francisco.
» Ulrich, D. (1996) *Human Resources Champions: The Next Agenda for Adding Value and Delivering Results.* Harvard Business School Press, Boston.
» Ulrich, D., Huselid, M. and Becker, B. (2001) *The HR Scorecard.* Harvard Business School Press, Boston.
» Ulrich, D. (1998) "A new mandate for human resources," *Harvard Business Review,* January-February, www.hbsp.harvard.edu/products/hbr/janfeb98/98111.html.

Other thinkers

Deming, W. Edwards – One of the key teachers behind the Japanese model; taught teamwork and overcoming fear. See Chapter 3, and *Motivation Express*.

Gratton, Lynda – Professor at the London Business School, she has also conducted research on links with business performance and writes on motivation and its centrality to business strategy in her latest book *Living Strategy*.[7] She features in "Key thinkers" in *Motivation Express*.

Huselid, Mark and Guest, David – from, respectively, Rutgers University, New Jersey, USA, and London School of Economics, UK; they have researched the links between approaches to people management and business success. See "Links with business performance," Chapter 9.

Legge, Karen – Professor of Management Studies at Warwick University, UK; she argues that much management thinking is overly deterministic, assuming that statements and objectives are enough to set one on the correct path. She analyses the gap between rhetoric and reality. Her analysis is similar to that of Henry Mintzberg, though focused more particularly on human resources practice.[8]

Mintzberg, Henry – Professor of Management Studies at McGill University in Montreal and Professor of Organization at INSEAD, he argues against the mechanistic assumptions of strategic planners and, as such, his theories place a higher priority on gaining the trust and commitment of staff.[9]

Morton, Clive – An independent training advisor and consultant, he is the author of *Becoming World Class* and *Beyond World Class*, which explain how to integrate people management and strategy in manufacturing companies (see Chapter 6).

Senge, Peter – The originator of the learning organization, he is an original thinker who argues that organizations are organic and unpredictable. He disapproves of the term "human resources," arguing that it downplays the centrality of people to success.[10]

NOTES

1 Goleman, D. (1995) *Emotional Intelligence*. Bantam, New York.

2 See www.intellectualcapital.se.

3 Schuler, R.S. and Jackson, S.E. (2001) "Turning knowledge into business advantage," *Financial Times*, January 15.

4 Schuler, R.S. and Jackson, S.E. (2001) "Human resource management: past, present and future," in *Comparative Labor Law and Industrial Relations* (7th edn). Kluwer Law International, The Hague.

5 Byrne, J.A. (1998) "How Jack Welch Runs GE," *Business Week*, August 6.

6 Ulrich, D. (1998) "A new mandate for human resources," *Harvard Business Review*, January–February (www.hbsp.harvard.edu/ products/hbr/janfeb98/98111.html).

7 Gratton, L. (2000) *Living Strategy*. FT/Prentice Hall, London.

8 Legge, K. (1995) *Human Resource Management: Rhetorics and Realities*. Macmillan, London.

9 Mintzberg, H. (1994) *The Rise and Fall of Strategic Planning*. Prentice Hall, London.

10 Senge, P. (1990) *The Fifth Discipline*. Doubleday, New York.

Resources for People Management

- » Personnel management associations
- » Consultancies
- » Journals
- » Books
- » Websites
- » Links with business performance

PERSONNEL MANAGEMENT ASSOCIATIONS

World Federation of Personnel Management Associations www.wfpma.com

The WFPMA is a global network of professionals in people management. It was founded in 1976 to aid the development and improve the effectiveness of professional people management all over the world. Its members are predominantly the national federations, which are made up of more than 50 national personnel associations representing over 300,000 people management professionals. Languages on the site are English, German, French and Spanish. The Japanese association can be contacted by English speakers via the US office of the Society for Human Resource Management (see below). The secretariat of the World Federation of Personnel Management Associations is currently the UK's Chartered Institute of Personnel and Development (www.cipd.co.uk).

The Society for Human Resource Management www.shrm.org

The Society for Human Resource Management is the voice of the human resource profession in the US. It provides education and information services, conferences and seminars, government and media representation, online services and publications to more than 165,000 professional and student members throughout the world. The Society is the world's largest human resource management association.

CONSULTANCIES

The Hay Group www.haygroup.com

The Hay Group is a global people management consultancy that offers direct advice to companies on pay, motivation, and other aspects of personnel. Its slogan of "People before Strategy" reflects an approach that sees the ways in which people work as the building block of a successful enterprise. It also produces a global compensation database.

The International Society for Performance Improvement www.ispi.org

Founded in 1962, the ISPI is an association dedicated to improving productivity and performance in the workplace. It represents more than 10,000 international and chapter members throughout the United States, Canada, and 40 other countries. ISPI's mission is to improve the functioning of organizations through people. Its members are primarily from the training and personnel professions.

The Saratoga Institute www.saratogainstitute.com

The Saratoga Institute specializes in developing tools to measure the impact and contribution of employees at an individual, team, and corporate level. It also advises companies on their approach to the management of people. The institute was founded by Jac Fitz-Enz, author of *The Return on Investment of Human Capital* (see "Books," below).

SHL www.shlsolutions.com

SHL, formerly known as Saville and Holdsworth, is a human resources consultancy with considerable expertise in selection and recruitment. But it also offers developmental tools, including a cultural audit.

Towers Perrin www.towers.com

Towers Perrin is advisor to around three-quarters of the world's largest companies, on the subjects of human resources management, communication, pay, and organizational effectiveness. It seeks to improve business performance through people.

Watson Wyatt www.watsonwyatt.com

Watson Wyatt brings people management and financial management together in its approach to consulting. It has developed the Human Capital Index, a measure of how well organizations motivate and use people, which it claims is predictive of business success (see "Links between motivation and the bottom line," below). It also provides consultancy on human resources policies to individual companies.

Links to a range of human resources organizations, with a UK and European focus, can be found at: www.personneltoday.net/pt_links/-links_listnew.asp.

The International Labor Organization www.ilo.org

Established in 1919, this is the branch of the United Nations that is dedicated to improving working conditions. It carries out research, holds conferences, and sets international standards to promote good employment practices.

JOURNALS

Most national personnel management associations publish national journals. These magazines deal with general and strategic matters for personnel managers, focusing both on organizational needs and on developmental needs of human resources professionals. They are generally monthly and include a news section. Examples are *People Management*, published by the Chartered Institute of Personnel and Development in the UK, and *Recursos Humanos*, published by the Venezuelan Asociacion de los Recursos Humanos (www.anri.org.ve). The national associations will also be able to help with journals and other materials on specialist issues such as pay, motivation, recruitment, teamwork, diversity, and so on.

In the English language there are journals that are independent of the associations, such as *Global HR* and *Personnel Today*, published by Reed Business Information (www.rbi.co.uk), and *Human Resource Executive* (www.hrexecutive.com). In the French language, *Le Figaro Economie*, a weekly supplement with the national newspaper, gives considerable coverage to human resources management.[1]

BOOKS

General and strategic human resources theory

Buckingham, M. *et al.* (2001) *Now, Discover Your Strengths!* Free Press, New York.

Deming, W. Edwards (1986) *Out of the Crisis*. Massachusetts Institute of Technology.

Fitz-Enz, J. and Phillips, J. (1999) *A New Vision for Human Resources: Defining the Human Resources Function by its Results*. Crisp Publications, New York.

Gratton, L. *et al.* (1999) *Strategic Human Resource Management*. Oxford University Press, Oxford.

Gratton, L. (2000) *Living Strategy*. FT/Prentice Hall, London.

Legge, K. (1995) *Human Resource Management: Rhetorics and Realities*. Macmillan, London.

Mintzberg, H. (1994) *The Rise and Fall of Strategic Planning*. Prentice Hall, London.

Morton, C. (1994) *Becoming World Class*. Macmillan Business, London.

Morton, C. (1996) *Beyond World Class*. Macmillan Business, London.

Pfeffer, J. (1994) *Competitive Advantage Through People*. Harvard Business School Press, Boston.

Pfeffer, J. (1998) *The Human Equation: Building Profits by Putting People First*. Harvard Business School Press, Boston.

Pfeffer, J. (2000) *Hidden Value: How Great Companies Achieve Extraordinary Results with Ordinary People*. Harvard Business School Press, Boston.

Schuler, R.S. and Jackson, S.E. (1999) *Strategic Human Resource Management: A Reader*. Blackwell, London.

Storey, J. (ed.) (1989) *New Perspectives on Human Resource Management*. Routledge, London.

Ulrich, D. and Lake, D. (1990) *Organizational Capability: Competing from the Inside Out*. Wiley, New York.

Ulrich, D., Ashkenas, R., Kerr, S. and Jick, T. (1995) *The Boundaryless Organization Breaking the Chains of Organization Structure*. Jossey-Bass, San Francisco.

Ulrich, D. (1996) *Human Resources Champions: The Next Agenda for Adding Value and Delivering Results*. Harvard Business School Press, Boston.

Ulrich, D., Huselid, M. and Becker, B. (2001) *The HR Scorecard: Linking People, Strategy and Performance*. Harvard Business School Press, Boston.

Websites

HR book summaries can be located at the sites below; for Websites of strategic HR consultants, see "Consultancies," above.

www.go2e-hr.com/new_page_10.htm – list of human resources titles from e-hr.com.

www.booksforbusiness.com – large selection of business titles from Toronto-based Books for Business.

www.cupahr.org/Hrpubs/reviews.html – list of human resources books from US universities' Website.

A guide to general management books, including sections on human resources and leadership, can be found at the American Management Association at:

www.amanet.org/books/index.htm.

Total quality

Akao, Y. (ed.) (1991) *Hoshin Kanri: Policy Deployment for Successful TQM* (originally published as *Hoshin kanri katsuyo no jissai*, 1988). Productivity Press, Cambridge MA.

Bechtell, M.L. (1996) *The Management Compass: Steering the Corporation Using Hoshin Planning* (an American Management Association management briefing). AMA Membership Publications Division, New York.

Ouchi, W. (1981) *Theory Z: How American Business Can Meet the Japanese Challenge*. Addison-Wesley, Boston.

Article

Kano, N. (1993) "A Perspective on Quality Activities in American Firms," *California Management Review*, **35** (3), 12–31.

Websites

www.deming.eng.clemson.edu/pub/den/deming_about.htm – Web site of the Deming Electronic Network, dedicated to encouraging the adoption of the ideas of W. Edwards Deming.

www.aqp.org – the site for the Association for Quality and Participation.

www.deming.org – home page of the W. Edwards Deming Institute.

www.worldbestquality.com – Website for the quality movement.

Intellectual capital and balanced scorecard

Edvinsson, L. and Malone, M. (1997) *Intellectual Capital*. HarperCollins, New York.

Fitz-Enz, J. (2000) *The ROI of Human Capital*. Amacom, New York.

Lev, B. (2001) *Value-driven Intellectual Capital: How to Convert Intangible Corporate Assets into Market Intangibles: Management, Measurement and Reporting*. Brookings Institution Press, Washington DC.

Sullivan, P. (2000) *Value*. Wiley, New York.

Sveiby, K-E. and Risling, A. (1986) *The Know-How Company (Kunskapsforetaget)*. Liber, Stockholm.

Sveiby, K-E. *et al.* (1989) *The Invisible Balance Sheet*. Ledarskap, Stockholm.

Articles

Kaplan, R.S. and Norton, D.P. (1992) "The balanced scorecard – measures that drive performance," *Harvard Business Review*, January–February, 71-9.

Kaplan, R.S. and Norton, D.P. (1996) "Using the balanced scorecard as a strategic management system," *Harvard Business Review*, January–February, 75-85.

Websites

www.sveiby.com – Website dedicated to the ideas of Karl-Erik Sveiby, pioneer of intellectual capital.

www.balancedscorecard.com – Website to help people implement the balanced scorecard approach.

www.bscol.com – Website to help people implement the balanced scorecard approach.

www.intellectualcapital.se – Website of the organization of the same name, which carries out independent intellectual capital assessments of organizations.

www.skandia.com – home page of the Swedish life assurance company Skandia, the first company to produce an intellectual capital report.

www.skandiafuturecenter.com – home page of the Future Center of Skandia, dedicated to pursuing the ideas of intellectual capital.

www.entovation.com – information and tools on knowledge management from Entovation.

www.skyrme.com – information, publications list and advice on knowledge management, by David Skyrme Associates.

Emotional intelligence

Gardner, H. (1993) *Multiple Intelligences*. BasicBooks, New York.

Goleman, D. (1995) *Emotional Intelligence*. Bantam, New York.

Articles

Ashforth, B.E. and Humphrey, R.H. (1995) "Emotion in the workplace: a reappraisal," *Human Relations*, **48** (2), 97–125.

Mayer, J.D. and Salovey, P. (1993) "The intelligence of emotional intelligence," *Intelligence*, 17, 433–42.

Websites

www.eq.org – Internet directory of Websites dedicated to emotional intelligence.

www.eiconsortium.org – Website for organizations in the Emotional Intelligence Consortium.

www.eqi.org – site dedicated to emotional intelligence, by Steve Hein.

www.equniversity.com – online campus for training materials on emotional intelligence.

The learning organization

Argyris, C. (1993) *On Organizational Learning*. Blackwell, Cambridge, MA.

Covey, S. (1989) *The Seven Habits of Highly Effective People*. Fireside, New York.

Kline, P. and Saunders, B. (1993) *Ten Steps to a Learning Organization*. Great Ocean Publishers, Virginia.

Senge, P. (1990) *The Fifth Discipline*. Doubleday, New York.

Senge, P. *et al*. (1994) *The Fifth Discipline Fieldbook*. Doubleday, New York.

Vail, P. (1996) *Learning as a Way of Being*. Jossey-Bass, San Francisco.

Articles

Argyris, C. (1991) "Teaching smart people how to learn," *Harvard Business Review*, May–June, 99–109.

Argyris, C. (1998) "Empowerment: the emperor's new clothes," *Harvard Business Review*, May–June, 98–105.

Leonard, D. and Straus, S. (1997) "Putting your company's whole brain to work," *Harvard Business Review*, July–August, 111–21.

Websites

www.learning-org.com - information on how to become a learning organization.

www.SoLonline.org/ - the site of the Society for Organizational Learning.

www.ustrategies.com - home page for University Strategies, a consulting firm for universities and colleges, which offers information on learning organizations.

www.ica-usa.org/WebLinks/weblink.html#orglrn - information on how to become a learning organization.

www.efmd.be - home page for European Foundation for Management Development.

LINKS WITH BUSINESS PERFORMANCE

Proving the case for better, or different, or more integrated approaches to the management of people in organizations has never been more strongly demanded by senior business leaders. A common complaint by general managers made of human resources professionals is that they fail to provide a sufficiently rigorous business case for the training, recruitment, or appraisal schemes that they may wish to introduce (see Chapter 6, "People move center-stage" and Chapter 8, "Adding value"). Many people in business - general managers and personnel professionals alike - are unaware of the wealth of research that indicates a strong correlation between the right human resources practices and business success. This can help people put together a business case; it can also furnish advice on which interventions may be more effective in different workplaces. Seven of the research studies are summarized below (they are also summarized in *Motivation Express*).

London Business School

The long-term, longitudinal, leading edge research by the London Business School reported that there was serious damage to motivation and to performance in the companies that had experienced more sudden and drastic reorganizations. There was less disruption, and better performance, at Hewlett Packard and Suchard Jacobs Kraft, where change was less abrupt and the integration of people processes into business was ingrained.

See Gratton, L. *et al.* (1999) *Strategic Human Resource Management*. Oxford University Press, Oxford.

University of Sheffield; London School of Economics; Chartered Institute of Personnel & Development

This study, published in 1997, based on research into medium-sized manufacturing companies by the Institute of Personnel & Development, along with the University of Sheffield and the London School of Economics, shows a close correlation between staff commitment and better performance on a range of "hard" measures, including profitability. Human resources were by far the most influential, explaining 19 percent of the variation in profitability compared with research and development, which registered 6 percent, and technology, which accounted for just 1 percent.

See Patterson, M. *et al.* (1997) *Impact of People Management Practices on Business Performance*, Chartered Institute of Personnel & Development.

Mark Huselid's work at Rutgers University
www.rci.rutgers.edu/~huselid/

Mark Huselid has been studying the relationship between a company's personnel policies and its business performance for many years. He has found that the firms that make development of their people a fully strategic goal perform spectacularly better than others. Practices that encourage people to behave in a way that supports the organization's goals are effective.

Watson Wyatt's Human Capital Index
www.watsonwyatt.com

The international consultancy Watson Wyatt has completed two thorough surveys of human resources practices at major companies – one in North America and one in Europe. It concluded that commitment to good practices in employing people adds up to 30 percent in total return to shareholders over a five-year period.

Successful features are:

» recruiting excellence;
» a collegial, flexible workplace;
» clear pay awards and accountability;
» clear and honest communication; and
» prudent use of resources.

Hay Group: culture change and business performance

This study has focused more on the quality of individual leaders within organizations. A summary of the findings of Hay research is written in *People Management*, June 28, 2001, which is published by the Chartered Institute of Personnel and Development. The author of this article was Chris Watkin of Hay, who can be contacted on chris_watkin@haygroup.com.

The Gallup Organization
www.gallupjournal.com/GMJarchive/issue1/
2001315i.asp

The Gallup Organization has carried out some comprehensive question-naire-based surveys in recent years. One report on the findings reads: "We collected employee engagement scores and business unit outcome data, such as profitability, sales, employee retention, customer satisfaction, for 7,939 business units, teams or workgroups in 36 companies ... The correlation was positive: highly engaged individuals were most often found in the high-performance units."

ENDNOTE

1 See, for example, "La grande mutation des ressources humaines," *Figaro Economie*, March 26, 2001.

Ten Steps to Making People Management Work

» Take a strategic view.
» Make a decision on measuring human capital.
» People matters are at the heart of restructuring, merging or down-sizing.
» Become a learning organization.
» Benchmark against principles, not numbers.
» Treat diversity as a feature of globalization, not a question of legal compliance.
» Do not use the trade unions as an alibi.
» Use information systems to their best effect.
» Work with other departments.
» Remember that people comprise the organization; they are not subordinate to it.

1. TAKE A STRATEGIC VIEW

This entails analyzing where the skills and expertise lie in the organization, what the organization's aims are, and seeking to ensure a close alignment between the respective aims of members of staff and of the senior managers. Many attempts to improve the management of people fail because they begin with the solution and do not analyze the real needs of the business (see Chapter 6, "People move center-stage").

For example, instead of researching the latest online training courses and insisting that all call center staff spend so many hours a week on them, the approach should be to carry out research of customers and identify areas where service could be improved in line with the objectives of the business. The next task is to research data on customer and employee retention, and construct an argument based on approximate cost savings from improving these indicators that can be sold to the board. Finally, one should consult with staff as to how such tailored training can best be delivered to overcome the weaknesses, and seek to redress staff shortages if there are any.

This approach highlights developmental needs for individual managers. In the case of people with a personnel management background, a business studies course, or finance for non-finance managers, or even an MBA, can provide not only greater awareness of business strategies, but also the confidence to present an argument in terms that are readily accepted and understood by other managers. In turn it is helpful if people with an accountancy background learn the importance of managing people, and the basics of teamwork and communication skills.

2. MAKE A DECISION ON MEASURING HUMAN CAPITAL

There is more than one way of attempting to gauge the relative strength of human capital in an organization. It is not an essential task, but what is important is to recognize that the vast bulk of value in the company is not recorded by conventional accounting. So, if there is no measure, there does have to be an acknowledgement of these invisible assets when taking decisions.

If one does decide to measure then one has to choose which measure to use: the intellectual capital measure (from intellectualcapital.se) and the balanced scorecard (from balancedscorecard.com) are the two most obvious. Jac Fitz-Enz, founder of the Saratoga Institute, has produced a similar measure,[1] along with the international consultancy Watson Wyatt (see Chapter 6 and Chapter 9).

Conventional accounting is around 500 years old, and it measures only transactions incurring costs, and fixed assets. At best it can only give a partial, and backward-looking, view of an organization's activities, and successful companies – even where they do not use formal measures of human capital or intellectual capital – take a broad range of factors into account in strategic management, rather than just those which are easiest to measure.

3. PEOPLE MATTERS ARE AT THE HEART OF RESTRUCTURING, MERGING OR DOWNSIZING

Redundancy programs seem to be an inevitable feature of the global economy and, while many mergers and restructurings are made for the wrong reasons, it is also true that no organization can remain organizationally static, given the relentless rise of new technology, new competitors, and changes to customer needs. Restructurings often fail not because they were illogical in concept, but because the people expected to carry them out were not sufficiently involved and/or felt their own careers were threatened by the changes and as a result were demotivated. This emerges in the leading edge research by the London Business School,[2] and also in research by the UK-based Roffey Park Management Institute and by Cranfield University.[3] Other research by Roffey indicates that mergers often have similarly disruptive effects.[4]

More effective approaches to change build on the principle set out in Step 2, above, which is that people represent the bulk of assets to the company, and that negative effects on this asset should at the very least be taken into account. They can outweigh the apparent savings from economies of scale in a merger, or reduced salary bill in a downsizing exercise. Moreover, the negative effects can last for years.

This means that the welfare, retention, and development of people – and communication with staff – need to be considered throughout any change program, rather than be tagged on at the end. See case studies, Chapter 7.

4. BECOME A LEARNING ORGANIZATION

Markets change rapidly, and organizations need to adapt. It is, however, more important to make the right change than the most rapid change. A true learning organization, in which employees are committed to continually developing and improving the service, will seek to adapt itself to meet the needs of the customers; if it is also innovative, it will anticipate the customers' desires. The key to this is to arrive at a stage where staff members are ambitious for the organization and for the customers, and in equal measure the organization's leaders are ambitious for the staff members and their goals.

The question of being a learning organization applies individually as well as collectively, and for the top management team as well as the technical staff or customer relations staff. Many executives neglect their own development and can become overly concerned with strategic positioning and relations with investors. Increasingly there is a need for managers to imitate the concept of "continuous professional development" that many public sector professionals, especially in the health services, have embraced. This sees learning as continuous, and sees adaptation to real working situations as being every bit as educational as a training course – though it also encourages active involvement in formal learning as well as in the workplace, so that the two go together. See "Learning organizations," Chapter 8.

5. BENCHMARK AGAINST PRINCIPLES, NOT NUMBERS

Mechanistic benchmarking often yields useless data, yet it remains a common practice. As the independent human resources consultant Paul Kearns comments, "Most of the data completed in benchmarking measures, for example number of training days per employee, are of no great interest to anyone outside the human resources department. Yet when more meaningful measures are used (profitability per employee, for instance) the database shows no causal connection to HR activity."

He goes on to chronicle the "worst possible piece of data that an HR department can collect," which is the full-time equivalents per HR department staff member, inviting the question whether 100-1 is better than 50-1. "Surely it depends on what the '1' HR person is doing?" he asks.[5]

What matter in people management are clarity of thinking, honesty in communication, and a genuine linking of people development programs to the needs of customers. Take the three case studies in Chapter 7: superficially, they appear very different. They are from different management models and different cultures. The Japanese firm Komatsu has its roots in the post-war theories of teamwork, quality, and knowledge sharing; the Swedish firm Skandia in the much newer technique of intellectual capital, while Southwest Airlines possesses the US concern with the quality of service. Skandia goes to enormous lengths to measure human capital; Southwest Airlines does not bother at all.

But in matters of important principle, the three have strong similarities. All integrate people development with organizational development; all encourage staff members to learn about the customers and improve their lives. Senior managers will communicate honestly: none of the three firms will spring unpleasant surprises on the staff; none of them will regard employees as being a cost, or a drain on the enterprise. Matters such as training and recruitment, which are regarded as chores in many other organizations, are given very high priority in these three.

6. TREAT DIVERSITY AS A FEATURE OF GLOBALIZATION, NOT A QUESTION OF LEGAL COMPLIANCE

The worst trap that managers can fall into when dealing with personnel matters is to look first at the law, and set policies according to minimum standards under the belief that anything more is a cost to the business. This is especially the case with equal opportunities. Increasingly an organization's customers and employees are recruited globally; and even if the spread is not so broad geographically, the increase in migration in recent years means that most local markets are ethnically diverse. This means that a diverse workforce helps attract new custom.

Another benefit of a diverse workforce is the breadth of experience and insight that it brings. No two peoples have the same way of looking at a problem.

Anti-discrimination laws have become stronger in most parts of the world, and in the USA, which sets most management trends, there have been high compensation pay-outs where courts have ruled that black and other minority people were disadvantaged in, for example, promotion opportunities. The best way to prevent this is to be genuine in embracing equal opportunities. Any sense that compliance with a law is minimal, or grudging, is likely to produce cynical feelings in the workplace that makes litigation more, not less, likely. The same general principle applies to avoiding disputes with trade unions (see Step 7, below).

See www.raceforopportunity.co.uk.

7. DO NOT USE THE TRADE UNIONS AS AN ALIBI

It is an approximate rule of thumb that an organization has the employee relations that its top management deserves. However, there can be unusual political circumstances, and in the 1960s and 1970s it was common for Trotskyite sects to infiltrate trade unions with the explicit aim of stirring up trouble on the factory floor. Even in these cases, however, such activists will find it difficult if there are no genuine grievances that they can rally people to.

If employee relations are poor then it is at least partly the fault of management. Features such as once-yearly negotiations, brinkmanship, and recourse to lawyers by both the management and union sides are symptoms of poor working relationships and low productivity, which no amount of legal reforms or weakening of trade unions can solve.

There are some signs that executives are learning this lesson. In the 1980s in the airline industry, for example, Frank Lorenzo was cheered by investors and the business press for his hostile treatment of the unions at Continental Airlines, even though his business record was poor. A decade later at British Airways Robert Ayling was ousted at least in part because of a prolonged strike in 1997, while his replacement Rod Eddington was head-hunted partly for his people management skills (see Chapter 6).

From the trade union side, there are fewer motives to be obstructive than in previous decades. The reduction of protected markets and monopolies means that employment is threatened if a company is not doing well, and this, together with more moderate politics, has encouraged the partnership movement. Personnel management organizations and human resources consultancies can offer advice with particular difficulties (see Chapter 9).

8. USE INFORMATION SYSTEMS TO THEIR BEST EFFECT

As well as learning about the business objectives, personnel professionals need to understand the latest technology, and what it can do. Most advances in technology in the past ten years have been concerned with communication, which has become markedly quicker and more convenient.

The most obvious changes in people management have concerned the transformation of the personnel function itself, as automated, self-entry data systems have been implemented across the economy since the mid 1990s.

The understanding by human resource professionals must go wider, however. It is important to know the different ways in which customers may want to use products and services; to consider and discuss whether, or to what extent, for example, the Internet may replace call centers. And recruiters should know which are the programming languages that are most likely to be needed in the short term and further into the future.

Technology can help teams work together. Internet chat groups, for example, are used to keep people of the same discipline at an international organization in touch with each other (see IBM case study, Chapter 4).

9. WORK WITH OTHER DEPARTMENTS

Financial control, marketing, and IT are not the enemies of those entrusted with people management. Organizations with strong departments can lack sufficient common cause. As discussed in Chapter 2, people management does not sit easily into the departmental structure, because it is something that every manager does. Personnel professionals therefore need to understand the contributions of other specialisms within the organization.

Greater mutual understanding is also the key to making a business case for more or different training, appraisal, or recruitment activities. By understanding the disciplines of financial control, for example, someone charged with people management can make a more robust case, and construct a proposed course of action in terms of investment with an expected return.

Broader cross-functional teams can work well. Many successful organizations, such as GlaxoWellcome (now part of GlaxoSmithKline), have deliberately introduced teamworking across disciplines, and prepared for it by training line managers in teamworking skills and introducing team-related bonuses.[6]

10. REMEMBER THAT PEOPLE COMPRISE THE ORGANIZATION; THEY ARE NOT SUBORDINATE TO IT

The war for talent that gripped many employers at the end of the 1990s reminded managers that employees are volunteers, not conscripts. Yet the basic model for much managerial action and thinking is scientific management, developed by Frederick Taylor and Henry Ford a century ago, in which employees are seen as being there solely to do the boss's bidding, to be kept in line with punishment and reward. Even some employers that do not formally hold to such principles have a tendency to react to economic downturn by hastily announcing redundancies and withholding information from staff about the condition of the company.

While it is difficult to rule out redundancies, as the Japanese experience has shown (see Chapter 3 and Chapter 6), the wider lesson is that people are not commodities, and attempts to treat them as such have proved ineffective (see Step 3, above). Moreover, people behave less and less like inanimate commodities as skill requirements and competition increase, and the business cycle has only time-limited effect – which means that short-term "savings" from redundancies can be quickly wiped out by consequent staffing difficulties when trading conditions improve.

People comprise the organization, and they are complex. Not only do they bring skills, which can be developed or which can erode, but they bring contacts and a network. They are the only link with customers, and they can choose to leave at any time. Management thinker Charles Handy may have been overly bullish in his forecast of the "portfolio career" made in the 1990s – where talented individuals have a range of skills and sell themselves to the most appropriate bidder – but it is certainly true that the monolithic organization expecting loyalty from its staff has broken down. Use of freelancers and joint ventures has increased, such that many organizations resemble a network of inter-locking relationships, rather than a hierarchical institution. Attention to the importance of these relationships and commitment to making an employer attractive to the right people now form a central managerial task.

KEY LEARNING POINTS

» People development should be integral to strategy and established in a way that helps the organization's aims, including those going through restructurings.

» If the organization does not wish to measure non-visible assets, it at least has to take them into account when making strategic decisions.

» In people management the important benchmarks concern principles, not processes or numbers.

» Diversity, employee consultation, and family-friendly hours should be entered into from a business perspective, respecting the wishes of employees as far as possible. Approaches based on the legal minimum can backfire.

» Technology has to be fully understood to be used in the most helpful way.

» The most important principle is that people comprise the organization.

NOTES

1 Fitz-Enz, J. (2000) *The ROI of Human Capital*. Amacom, New York.
2 Gratton, L. *et al*. (1999) *Strategic Human Resource Management*. Oxford University Press, Oxford.
3 Holbeche, L. (1997) *Career Management in Flatter Structures*. Butterworth Heinemann, London; and Sahdev, K. *et al*. (2001) Creating a Resilient Workforce. Cranfield University/Pearson, London.
4 Garrow, V. *et al*. (2000) *Strategic Alliances – Getting the People Bit Right*. Roffey Park, Horsham, UK.
5 Kearns, P. (2001) "HR benchmarking is more than cost-cutting," *Personnel Today*, July 17.
6 Gratton, L. (2000) *Living Strategy*. Prentice Hall, London.

Frequently Asked Questions (FAQs)

Q1: What is the difference between personnel and human resources?

A: See Chapter 2 for an explanation.

Q2: Why do human resources professionals not make a business case for their plans?

A: See "The modern paradox," Chapter 6, and "Links with business performance," Chapter 9.

Q3: Does the failure of the Japanese model of lifetime employment mean that the Western model is more appropriate?

A: See "Have the Japanese and German partnerships run their course?" and "No return to hire and fire," Chapter 6.

Q4: Does the increasing amount of labor regulation mean that people management is better done by lawyers?

A: See "Employee consultation, the unions and family-friendly policies," Chapter 6.

Q5: Does the spread of automated personnel systems mean that personnel management is better outsourced to specialist suppliers?

A: See Chapter 4 for a discussion on this topic.

Q6: What do intellectual capital and knowledge management have to do with people management?

A: See "Intellectual capital," Chapter 6; "Make a decision on measuring human capital," Chapter 10; and the Skandia case study, Chapter 7.

Q7: Are we likely to see a global, flexible labor market?

A: See Chapter 5 for a discussion on this topic.

Q8: Should strategic positioning and return to shareholders take precedence over employee welfare?

A: See Chapter 1; "The modern paradox," Chapter 6; case studies, Chapter 7; and "Links with business performance," Chapter 9.

Q9: Can employee welfare and development be maintained during redundancy programs and restructurings?

A: See "People matters are at the heart of restructuring, merging or downsizing," Chapter 10.

Q10: Does the new economy change the rules for employee relations?

A: See "Dotcoms and the new economy," Chapter 4.

Index